Mary A. (Mary Artemisia) Lathbury

Bible Heroes

Stories from the Bible

Mary A. (Mary Artemisia) Lathbury

Bible Heroes
Stories from the Bible

ISBN/EAN: 9783743323445

Manufactured in Europe, USA, Canada, Australia, Japa

Cover: Foto ©Lupo / pixelio.de

Manufactured and distributed by brebook publishing software (www.brebook.com)

Mary A. (Mary Artemisia) Lathbury

Bible Heroes

BIBLE HEROES

Stories from the Bible

BY

MARY A. LATHBURY

WITH INTRODUCTION BY

BISHOP JOHN H. VINCENT

ILLUSTRATED

WITH NUMEROUS FULL-PAGE COLORED PLATES,
AND PHOTO-ENGRAVINGS

BOSTON
DeWOLFE, FISKE & CO.

PREFACE.

To Mothers.

I HAVE been asked to prepare this little aid for your use in the Home—that first and greatest of schools. The school was founded by the Maker of men, and He called mothers to be its earliest and most important teachers. He prepared a text-book for it which we call His Word, illustrating it richly and fully from life and Nature, and filling it with His Spirit. Wherever it is known, as the children become the members of the Church, the citizens of the State, the people of the World, the Book goes with them, forming the Church, the State, the World. It is not only equal to the need, but contains infinite riches that wait to be unveiled.

That no busy mother may say, "I cannot take time to gather from the Bible the simple lessons that my children need," this book of little stories—together making one—has been written. I have tried to preserve the pure outlines of the sacred record from the vivid description and the suggestive supposition that are sometimes introduced to add charm to the story, and in all quoted speech I have used the exact words of the authorized version of the Scriptures, so that the earliest impression made upon the memory of the child might be one that should remain.

The stories are not a substitute for the Word—only little approaches to it through which young feet may be guided by her who holds a place next to the great Teacher in His work with little children.

M. A. L.

INTRODUCTION.

WHEN the children gather at mother's knee, and the tiniest finds a place in mother's arms, and all clamor for a "story," "a story, mamma," how lovely is the picture—the living picture—that circle makes! Love, longing, wisdom, expectancy, faith, shining eyes, lips that move involuntarily, keeping time to the sweet movements of mother's lips! Blessed group! Happy mother!

When the stories mother tells are light and meaningless, full of rhyme and rollick, even their eyes are bright and faces radiant, and her own sweet face and voice give charm and weight and significance to the delicious nonsense she rehearses.

Why not give to this receptive and eager audience stories full of deepest meaning, facts, parables, myths charged with *truth?* Why not people little memories with heroes, saints, kings, prophets, apostles? Why not give stories to story-loving youngsters that will turn into immortal pictures and be transformed some day into living factors in the making of character? And why not give them as comparison the babe of Bethlehem, the boy of Nazareth, the lad of twelve years in the schools of the Temple, the man of gentle love, the preacher of righteousness, the worker of heavenly wonders, the Son of Man, the Son of God, the Prince of Peace?

The Book of books is the children's Book. It is a story book. And the stories are "true stories." And the lessons to be drawn from them are numberless, and will come up out of the treasure-house of memory when mother's eyes are closed and her voice silent.

It is a great thing to put mother and the Book together in Baby's thought; in the big boy's memory; in the grown-up man's heart and life.

This book is mother's book; to aid her in doing the best and most lasting work a mother can do to sow seed and set out vines the branches of which shall reach into the world of spirits, and from which she and her children may long afterwards pluck fruit together in the eternal kingdom.

JOHN H. VINCENT.

CHAUTAUQUA, 1898.

CONTENTS.

CHAPTER.		PAGE.
I.	THE BEGINNING OF THINGS	1
II.	THE GREAT FLOOD	4
III.	ABRAHAM—THE FATHER OF THE FAITHFUL	7
IV.	ISAAC, THE SHEPHERD PRINCE	14
V.	JACOB, A PRINCE OF GOD	16
VI.	JOSEPH, THE CASTAWAY	22
VII.	JOSEPH, A SERVANT, A PRISONER AND A SAINT	25
VIII.	JOSEPH, THE SAVIOR OF HIS PEOPLE	28
IX.	THE CRADLE THAT WAS ROCKED BY A RIVER	35
X.	MOSES IN MIDIAN	38
XI.	THE ROD THAT TROUBLED EGYPT	39
XII.	FOLLOWING THE CLOUD	44
XIII.	IN THE BORDERS OF CANAAN	52
XIV.	A NATION THAT WAS BORN IN A DAY	54
XV–XVI.	SAMSON, THE STRONG	58
XVII.	RUTH	62
XVIII.	SAMUEL—THE CHILD OF THE TEMPLE	66
XIX.	THE MAKING OF A KING	69
XX.	THE SHEPHERD BOY OF BETHLEHEM	72
XXI.	THE POWER OF A PEBBLE	74
XXII.	FAITHFUL UNTO DEATH	76
XXIII.	DAVID, THE OUTCAST	79

CONTENTS.

CHAPTER.		PAGE.
XXIV.	EVERY INCH A KING	82
XXV.	DAVID'S SIN	84
XXVI.	DAVID'S SORROW	86
XXVII.	THE BUILDING OF THE GOLDEN HOUSE	92
XXVIII.	ELIJAH, THE GREAT HEART OF ISRAEL	97
XXIX.	THE LITTLE CHAMBER ON THE WALL	104
XXX.	A LITTLE MAID OF ISRAEL	108
XXXI.	THE TWO BOY KINGS	109
XXXII.	THE FOUR CAPTIVE CHILDREN	111
XXXIII.	THE MASTER OF THE MAGICIANS	116
XXXIV.	THE STORY OF JONAH	121
XXXV.	ESTHER, THE QUEEN	125

COLORED ILLUSTRATIONS.

REBEKAH	Frontispiece	
RETURN OF THE DOVE	Opposite Page	1
JACOB'S DREAM	" "	16
JOSEPH SOLD INTO EGYPT	" "	26
THE FINDING OF MOSES	" "	36
RUTH GLEANING	" "	62
THE CHILD OF THE TEMPLE	" "	66
THE SHEPHERD BOY OF BETHLEHEM	" "	70
THE POWER OF A PEBBLE	" "	76
SAUL ATTEMPTS THE LIFE OF DAVID	" "	86
THE FEEDING OF ELIJAH	" "	104
DANIEL IN THE LIONS' DEN	" "	114

RETURN OF THE DOVE.

BIBLE HEROES.

STORIES FROM THE BIBLE.

CHAPTER I.

THE BEGINNING OF THINGS.

AWAY back in the beginning of things God made the sky and the earth we live upon. At first it was all dark, and the earth had no form, but God was building a home for us, and his work went on through six long days, until it was finished as we see it now.

On the first day God said, "Let there be light," and the black night turned to gray, and light came. God called the light Day, and the darkness Night, and the evening and the morning made the first day.

Then God divided the waters, so that there were clouds above and seas below, and He called the clouds heaven. It was the second day.

Then the seas were gathered together by themselves, and the dry land rose above them, and God saw that it was good. Then He called to the grass, and the plants, and the trees to come out of the ground, and they came bearing their seeds, and He called the third day good.

Then God called to the two great lights, the sun and the moon, to shine clear in the sky, which had been first dark, and then gray, and they rose and set to make day and night, and seasons and years, and the stars came also, and it was the fourth day.

Then God called for all kinds of fishes that swim in the seas, and rivers, and for all kinds of birds that fly in the air, and they came, and it was the fifth day.

And then God called for the animals to live on the green earth, and the cattle and the great beasts, and the creeping things came, and God called them all good.

After this he made the first of the great family of Man. He made them after His own likeness. He made their bodies from the earth, but their souls He breathed into them, so that Man is a spirit, living in an earthly body, and can understand about God and love Him. He blessed them and told them to become many, and to rule over all the earth, with its beasts and birds, and fishes, and it was the sixth day.

The Man's name was Adam, and the woman, who was made from a piece of Adam's body nearest to his heart, was named Eve.

Then God's world was finished, and on the seventh day there was rest. God was pleased with all that was made, and He made the seventh day holy, by setting it apart from all the others. We keep the Sabbath, or the Lord's day still, in which his children may rest and worship.

Adam and Eve were very happy, for they had never done anything wrong. God gave them a beautiful wide garden, called Eden, full of flowers and all kinds of fruit, and with a river flowing through it, and told Adam to take care of the garden, and He sent all the animals and birds to Adam to be named. God told him also that he might eat the fruit of all the trees of the garden except one—the tree of knowledge of good and evil—but if he ate of the fruit of that tree he should surely die, and Adam and Eve loved God, and had no wish to disobey Him, for He was their Father.

But there was a creeping serpent in the garden, and the evil spirit that puts wrong thoughts in our hearts spoke to Eve through the serpent.

"You shall not die," he said, "but you shall be wise like God if you will eat of this fruit," and Eve ate of the fruit, and gave it to her husband. Then they knew that they had sinned, and when they heard the voice of God in the garden calling them, they hid among the trees, for they were unhappy and afraid. When the Lord had asked Adam if he had eaten of the fruit that was forbidden, Adam laid the sin upon Eve, who gave it to him, and Eve said that the serpent had tempted her to eat of the fruit. God knew that they must suffer for their sin, so He sent them out of the garden to make a garden for themselves, and to work, and suffer pain, as all who came after them have done to this day; but He gave them a great promise, that among their children's children One should be born who would be stronger than sin, and a Savior from it.

After this two little children were sent to comfort Adam and Eve—first Cain, and then Abel. When they grew up Cain was a farmer, but Abel was a shepherd.

They had been taught to worship God by bringing the best of all they had to Him, and so Cain brought fruit and grain to lay upon his altar, but Abel brought a lamb.

DRIVEN FROM EDEN.

God looked into their hearts and saw that Abel wished to do right, but Cain's heart was full of sin. Cain was angry because the Lord was pleased with the worship of Abel, and while they talked in the field Cain killed his brother. When the Lord said to Cain, "Where is thy brother?" he answered, "I know not. Am I my brother's keeper?" And the Lord sent him away from home, to wander from place to place over the earth, and find no rest, but He promised that no one should hurt Cain, or kill him as he had killed his brother, so he went away into another land to live.

Adam lived many years after this and had other children, but at last he died, when his children's children were beginning to spread over the land.

CHAPTER II.

THE GREAT FLOOD.

As the people of the earth grew to be many more and spread over the plains and hills, they also grew very wicked. They forgot God, and all the thoughts of their hearts were evil. Only Noah still worshipped God and tried to do right.

The people had destroyed themselves, and so God said to Noah:

"The end of all flesh is come; make thee an ark of gopher wood."

He told Noah to make it of three stories, with a window in the top, and a door in the side. It was to be a great floating house, more than four hundred feet long and full of rooms, and it was to be covered with tar within and without, so that the water should not creep in.

"I bring a flood of waters upon the earth," said the Lord, "and everything that is in the earth shall die."

This was to be the house of Noah, with his wife, and his three sons and their wives, during the great flood.

Does the house seem large for eight people? God had told Noah to make room for a little family of every kind of bird and beast that lived, and to gather food of all kinds for himself and for them.

So Noah did all that the Lord had told him to do, and seven days before the great storm he heard the Lord calling:

"Come thou and all thy house into the ark," and that very day, Noah with his wife and his sons, Shem, Ham, and Japtheth, and their wives, went

THE GREAT FLOOD.

into their great black house, and through the window in the top came flying the little families of birds and insects, from the tiny bees and humming birds, to the great eagles, and through the door on the side came the famlies of animals, two by two, from the little mice to the tall giraffes, and the elephants, and when all had come the Lord shut them in.

It rained forty days and forty nights, and the waters rose higher and higher, covering the hills, and creeping up the mountains, so that every living thing died except Noah, and all that were with him in the ark.

But after ten months the tops of the mountains were seen, and Noah sent out a raven and a dove. The raven flew to and fro, but the dove came back into the ark, because she found no place to rest her foot.

After seven days Noah sent her out again, and she returned with an olive leaf in her bill, and then Noah knew that the waters were going away.

After seven days again he sent out his good little dove, and she did not come back. So Noah was sure that the earth was getting dry, and that God would soon tell him to go out of the ark.

And so he did. Think how glad the sheep and cows were to find fresh grass, and the birds to fly to the green trees.

What a silent world it must have been, for there were none but Noah and his family in all the earth. Noah did not forget how God had saved them, and he made an altar of stone, and offered beasts and birds as a sacrifice. When he looked up to the sky there was a beautiful rainbow. It was God's promise that there should be no more floods upon the earth. He still sends the rainbow to show us that He is taking care of this world, and will always do so.

Perhaps the people who lived after this—for Noah's children's children increased very fast—did not believe God's promise, for they began to build a great tower, or temple, on the plain of Shinar; or perhaps they had grown proud and wicked, and wanted a temple for the worship of idols; but the Lord changed their speech, so that they could not understand each other, and they were scattered over other countries; and so each country began to have a language of its own.

CHAPTER III.

ABRAHAM—THE FATHER OF THE FAITHFUL.

The people who lived four thousand years ago were very much like children who easily forget. They told their children about the great flood, but nearly all forgot to tell them of the good God who is the Father of us all, whom we should always love and obey. Yet there is always one, if not more, who remembers God, and keeps his name alive in the world.

Abram had tried to do right, though there was no Bible in the world then, and no one better than himself to help him but God, and one day He called Abram, and told him to go away from his father's house into another country.

"A land that I will show thee," said the Lord, "and I will make of thee a great nation."

He also made Abram a wonderful promise,—

"In thee shall all the families of the earth be blessed."

He meant that sometime the Savior should be born among Abram's children's children, and that He should be the Savior of all the nations of the earth.

Abram did just what God told him to do. He took Sarai, his wife, and Lot, his nephew, and some servants, and cows, and sheep, and camels, and asses, and went into the land of Canaan. When they rested at night Abram and Lot set some sticks in the ground, and covered them with skins for a tent, and near by they made an altar, where Abram offered a sacrifice, for that was the only way they could worship God when the earth was young.

Abram went down into Egypt when there was a lack of food in Canaan, but he came back to Bethel, where he made the altar before, and worshipped God there.

He was very rich, for his cattle and sheep had grown into great herds and flocks, though he had sold many in Egypt for silver, and gold, and food. Abram and Lot moved often, for their flocks and herds soon ate up the grass. Then they rolled up the tents, and loaded the camels and asses, and went where the grass was thick and fresh.

They could easily live in tents, for the country was warm. But Abram's herdsmen and Lot's herdsmen sometimes quarreled. And so Abram spoke kindly to Lot, and told him to take his servants, and flocks, and herds, and go where the pastures were good, and he would go the other way. So they parted, and Lot went to the low plains of the Jordan, but Abram went to the high plains of Mamre, in Hebron, and there he built another altar to the Lord, who had given him all that country—to him and to his children forever.

There were warlike people in Canaan, and once when they had carried off Lot from Sodom, Abram took his servants and herdsmen and went out to fight. He had more than three hundred men, and they took Lot away from the enemy, and brought him back to Sodom. It was here that Abram met a wonderful man, who was both a king and a priest. His name was Melchisedek, and he brought Abram bread and wine, and blessed him there.

After this, God spoke to Abram one evening, and promised that he should have a son, and then while Abram stood outside his tent, with the great sky thick with stars above him, God promised him that his children's children should grow to be as countless as the stars. That was hard to believe, but Abram believed God always and everywhere.

Still no child came to Abram and Sarai, and Abram was almost a hundred years old, but God spoke to him again, and told him that he should be the father of many nations.

He told Abram that a little boy would be born to them, and his name would be Isaac, and God changed Abram's name to Abraham, which means " Father of many people," and Sarai's to Sarah, which means " Princess."

Abraham was sitting in his tent one hot day, when three men stood by him. They were strangers, and Abraham asked them to rest beneath the tree, and bathe their feet, while he brought them food. So Sarah made cakes, and a tender calf was cooked, and these with butter, and milk, were set before the men. But they were not men of this world ; they were angels, and they had come to tell Abraham and Sarah once more that their little child was sure to come. Then the angels went away, but one of them, who must have been the Lord Himself in an angel's form, stopped to tell Abraham that He was going to destroy Sodom and Gomorrah, because the people who lived there were so very wicked, and Abraham prayed Him to spare them if even ten good men could be found in them, for he remembered that Lot lived in Sodom. But the Lord never forgets. The two angels went to Sodom and stayed with Lot until morning, when they took him and all his family outside the city, and then the Lord said to him, "Escape for thy life—look not behind thee, neither stay thou in all the plain."

THE THREE STRANGERS.

And the Lord hid them in the little town of Zoar, while a great rain of fire fell upon the wicked cities of the plain, until they became a heap of ashes. Only Lot's wife looked back to see the burning cities, and she became a pillar of salt.

The next morning when Abraham looked from Hebron down toward the cities of the plain, a great smoke was rising from them like the smoke of a furnace.

At last the Lord's promise to Abraham and Sarah came true. A little son was born to them, and they called him Isaac. They were very happy, for though Abraham was a hundred years old, no child had ever been sent them.

When he was about a year old they made a great feast for him, and all brought gifts and good wishes, yet the little lad Ishmael, the son of Hagar, Sarah's servant, mocked at Isaac. Sarah was angry, and told her husband that Hagar and her boy must be sent away. So he sent them out with only a bottle of water and a loaf of bread; for God had told Abraham to do as Sarah wished him to do, and He would take care of little Ishmael, and make him the father of another nation.

When the water was gone, and the sun grew very hot, poor Hagar laid her child under a bush to die, for she was very lonely and sorrowful. While she hid her eyes and wept, saying,

"Let me not see the death of the child," she heard a voice out of heaven telling her not to be afraid.

"Arise, lift up the lad," said the voice, "for I will make him a great nation."

And God opened her eyes to see a well of water near. Then she filled the empty bottle, and gave the boy a drink, and God took good care of them ever after, though they lived in a wilderness.

Ishmael grew up to be an archer, and became the father of the Arabs, who still live in tents as Ishmael did.

But the Lord let a strange trial come to the little lad Isaac, also. His father loved and obeyed God, but there were heathen people around them, who worshipped idols, and sometimes killed their own children as a sacrifice to these idols. Abraham brought the best of his lambs and cattle to offer to the Lord; but one day the Lord told Abraham to take his only son Isaac and offer him upon a mountain called Moriah as a burnt sacrifice to God. Abraham had always obeyed God, and believed his word, and now, though he could not understand, he rose up early in the morning and took his young son, with

HAGAR IN THE DESERT.

two servants, and an ass loaded with wood, to the place of which God had told him.

They were three days on the journey, but at last they came to the high place, where the city of Jerusalem was afterward built, and to the very rock upon which the temple was built long afterward, with its great altar and Holy of Holies.

Abraham had left the young men at the foot of the mount, and went with Isaac to the great rock on the top of the mount.

"My father," said Isaac, "where is the lamb for a burnt offering?"

"My son, God will provide himself a lamb for a burnt offering," said his father, still obeying God, and believing His word, that Isaac should be the father of many nations.

Abraham made an altar of stones, and bound Isaac and laid him upon it, but when his hand was lifted to offer up the boy, the Lord called to him from heaven. "Lay not thine hand upon the lad," said the voice, "for now I know that thou fearest God, seeing thou hast not withheld thine only son from me."

Then Abraham turned and saw a ram with its twisted horns caught in the bushes, and he offered it to the Lord instead of his son. How glad and grateful Abraham must have been that morning, when he came down the mountain, with Isaac walking beside him, to think that he had still obeyed God when it was hard to do so.

Abraham was an old man when Sarah died. They had lived together a long lifetime, and he mourned for her many days. He bought a field close by the oak-shaded plain of Mamre in Hebron, and there in a rocky cave he buried her. He was called a Prince of God by the Canaanites because he lived a true, faithful life.

A few years after he also went to God, and his body was laid beside Sarah's in the cave-tomb. Ishmael came up from the south country to mourn with Isaac at the burial of their father, the Friend of God, and Father of the faithful.

ON MOUNT MORIAH.

CHAPTER IV.

ISAAC THE SHEPHERD PRINCE.

Before Abraham died, he thought much about his dear son Isaac, to whom he was going to leave all that he had. The young man had no mother, no sister, and soon he would have no father. So the old man called his old and faithful servant, and told him to go on a journey into the land of his fathers, and bring back with him a wife for his son Isaac.

The children of Nahor, Abraham's brother, lived there still, and Abraham wished for his son Isaac a wife of his own people, who should be both good and beautiful, and not like the heathen women of Canaan.

So the old servant listened to Abraham and promised to do all that he commanded.

He loaded ten camels with presents for his master's family away in Syria, and Abraham said:

"The Lord shall send His angel before thee," and from his tent door he saw the little caravan of camels and servants, as they set out across the plain, toward the land beyond the river Jordan.

There was a desert to cross and many dangers to meet, but the old servant believed in the God his master worshipped, and was not afraid.

When he came to Haran, he stopped outside the town by a well of water. It was early evening, and the women were coming each with a water-jar on her shoulder, to draw water.

The old man prayed that the Lord would show him which among these daughters of the men of the city, was the one who was to be his young master's wife.

Before his prayer was ended, Rebekah, of the family of Abraham's brother Nahor, came bearing her pitcher on her shoulder. She looked very kind and beautiful, and when she had filled her pitcher, the old man asked her for a drink of water. Then she let down the pitcher upon her hand saying:

"Drink, my lord," and asked if she should also give water to his camels. While she was giving him a drink, the man showed her some golden jewels that he had brought, and when he had asked her name, and knew that God had sent her to him for his young master, he gave them to her, and worshipped the Lord who had led him to the house of his master's brother.

Then Rebekah ran in and told Laban, her brother, and the old servant of Abraham had a warm welcome at the door of Nahor's house.

"Come in, thou blessed of the Lord," they said.

And after they had cared for the camels and the men, there was a hurrying of servants to prepare a feast, but the old man would not taste food until he had given the message of his master. Then the father and brother of Rebekah, saw that the Lord had sent for her, and they said:

"Let her be thy master's son's wife, as the Lord hath spoken."

And the old servant bowed his face to the ground worshipping the Lord who had led him.

Then there was feasting and giving of costly gifts, and preparing to take a long journey, for the old servant was in haste to get back to his master, and Rebekah, who was willing to go, took her maid-servants and rode away into a far country to be the wife of Isaac.

When Isaac was walking in his field at sunset, thinking and praying to God, he looked up and saw that the camels were coming, and he hastened to meet them. When the old servant told Rebekah that it was his young master, she alighted from her camel, and covered herself with a long veil as was the custom of the Syrian women. When the old servant had told the story of his journey, he gave Rebekah to Isaac, and he took her to the tent that had been his mother's, and she became his wife, so that he was no longer lonely and sad.

Isaac lived to a very great age, and had two sons, Jacob and Esau. He was a gentle, quiet man, fond of his family, his flocks, and herds, and at the place where his father and mother were buried, he lived among the fields and oak groves of Hebron until he died.

CHAPTER V.

JACOB, A PRINCE OF GOD.

Jacob and Esau were the twin sons of Isaac and Rebekah.

They did not look alike as twins often do, and they were very unlike in all their ways. As they grew up, Esau loved the forests and wild places. He made bows and arrows, and was a hunter, and brought home wild birds and deer, for his father was very fond of such food. Jacob helped his father with the flocks, and learned how to cook food from his mother, who loved him more than she loved Esau.

One day Esau came home from hunting tired and hungry, and smelled the delicious soup of red lentils that Jacob was making. He begged Jacob to give him some, and Jacob, who wanted to be eldest, and have the right to the blessing that fathers gave to the first-born in those days, said :

"Sell me this day thy birthright," and Esau gave him all his rights as the first born, for a little food which he might have had as a free gift.

Jacob wanted to be counted in the great promise that God had given to Abraham, but Esau despised it.

Afterward, when Isaac was old and his eyes were dim, he called Esau, and asked him to go out into the fields and shoot a deer, and cook the venison that he loved, so that he might eat it and bless his first born before he died.

Rebekah heard it, and told Jacob to bring kids from the flock, which she cooked and served as venison. Then she dressed Jacob in the clothes of Esau, and told him to say that it was Esau who had brought the venison. Isaac said:

"The voice is the voice of Jacob," but he put his hands on him, and believed it was Esau, and blessed him.

When Esau came home and brought venison to his father, Isaac said :

"Who art thou?" and when Esau said, "I am thy son, thy first-born, Esau," the old man trembled, and told Esau the blessing had been given to another.

Poor Esau cried out with grief, "Hast thou but one blessing?" "Bless me, even me also, O my father."

(16)

JACOB'S DREAM.

And so Isaac blessed him, but he could not call back the blessing of the first-born. The Lord knew that Jacob would grow to be a good man, and love the things of God best, and that Esau would always love the things of this world best, yet it was wrong of Jacob and Rebekah to deceive, for we may not do evil that good may come.

After this Esau hated his brother, and said he would kill him.

So Isaac called Jacob, and, blessing him again, sent him away into Syria to the house of Laban, where Rebekah had lived, and where Abraham's servant went to find her for his master's son.

One night, when he was not far on his way, he lay down to sleep, with a stone for his pillow, on a hillside that looked toward his home, and he dreamed a wonderful dream. He saw a ladder reaching from earth to heaven, and a vision of angels who were going up and down upon it.

Above it stood the Lord, who spoke to Jacob, and gave to him the promise that He had first given to Abraham, and told him that He would go with him, and bring him again into his own land.

Jacob was afraid when he woke, for he had seen the heavens opened, and had heard God's voice. He made an altar of the pillow of stone, and called it Bethel—the House of God—and then he vowed that the Lord should be his God, and he added,—

"Of all that thou shalt give me, I will surely give a tenth unto thee."

When Jacob came to Haran, he saw the well from which his mother used to draw water. There were three flocks of sheep lying by it, waiting for all the flocks to gather in the cool of the day to be watered. Soon Rachel, the daughter of Laban, came leading her father's flocks, and one of the shepherds told Jacob whose daughter she was.

So Jacob rolled the stone from the well, and watered the flocks of Laban, his mother's brother. Then he kissed Rachel, and told her that he was Rebekah's son, and she ran and told her father.

There was great joy in Laban's house because Jacob had come, and after he had stayed a month with them Laban asked him to stay and take care of his flocks, and he would pay him for his work.

Since the day he had seen Rachel leading her father's flocks he had chosen her in his heart to be his wife. So he said that he would work for Laban seven years, if at the end of that time he would give him Rachel for his wife. Laban was quite willing to do so, and the seven years seemed to Jacob but a few days, for the love he had to Rachel. But, according to the custom of that country, the younger daughter could not be given in marriage

ISAAC BLESSING JACOB.

before the elder, and so Laban gave his daughter Leah also, and both Leah and Rachel became the wives of Jacob, for Jacob lived in that far away time and country of the early world when men were allowed to take more than one wife, and when each man was both king and priest over his family and tribe, and worshipped God by offering burnt sacrifices upon an altar.

After twenty years of work with Laban, in which he had earned many flocks and herds for himself, Jacob took his wives and the little sons God had sent him, and his flocks and herds, and started on a journey to his old home. Isaac was still alive, and Jacob longed to see him. He had lived long in Haran for fear of his brother Esau, and now he must travel through Edom, Esau's country, on his way to his old home.

As he was on his way some of God's angels met him, and he was strengthened. Still he feared Esau, and sent some of his men to tell his brother that he was coming.

The men came back, saying that Esau, with four hundred men, was coming to meet them.

Poor Jacob! He remembered the sin of his youth, when he had stolen the blessing from Esau, and he was afraid, and prayed God to protect him.

He sent his servants again to meet Esau with great presents of flocks, and herds, and camels, and after placing his wives and little ones in the safest place, he sent all that he had over the brook Jabbok, and he stayed on the other side to pray. It was as if he wrestled with a man all night, and when the day began to break the man wished to go, but Jacob said:

"I will not let thee go except thou bless me."

So the man blessed him there, and call his name Israel; "for as a prince," he said, "hast thou power with God and with men, and hast prevailed."

Then Jacob knew that the Lord Himself, in the form of a man, had been with him, and he had seen Him face to face.

And as the sun rose he passed over the brook. When he looked up he saw Esau and his men coming, and when he had told his family to follow him, he went straight before them, for he was no longer afraid to meet his brother.

Jacob's prayer had been answered, and Esau ran to meet his brother, and throwing his arms around him, wept on his shoulder. Then they talked in a loving and brotherly way, and Esau returned to his home with the presents Jacob had given him, and Jacob went on his way into Canaan full of joy and thankfulness. He stopped a little while in a pleasant place to rest his flocks and cattle, but he longed to see the place where he first saw the angels of

JACOB AND RACHAEL.

God, and heard the voice of the Lord blessing him, so they journeyed on to Beth-el, and there built an altar and worshipped God.

Again the Lord spoke to Jacob at Beth-el, and called him Israel, and blessed him.

After they left Beth-el, they came near to Bethlehem, where many hundred years afterward the Lord Jesus was born, and there another little son was born to Rachel, and there too God sent for her, and took her to Himself, and there her grave was made.

The little boy was named Benjamin, and was the youngest of Jacob's twelve sons, who became the fathers of the twelve tribes of Israel, and the princes of a great nation.

Jacob was almost home. His great family, with all the flocks and herds, had been long on the way, for they often spread their tents by the brooks in the green valleys, that the cattle might rest and find pasture, but at last the long caravan came slowly over the fields of Mamre to Hebron, and Isaac, whom the Lord had kept alive to see his son once more, was there in his tent waiting for him.

But soon after this he died, an hundred and eighty years old, and Esau came, and the two brothers laid their father in the cave that Abraham bought when Sarah died, and where he had buried Rebekah, and Jacob became patriarch in place of his father.

CHAPTER VI.

JOSEPH, THE CASTAWAY.

Of all the sons of Jacob, Joseph and Benjamin were the dearest to him, because they were the sons of his beloved Rachel, who had died on the journey from Syria into Canaan. They were also the youngest of all the twelve sons. When Joseph was about seventeen years old, he sometimes went with his elder brothers to keep his father's flocks in the fields. He wore a long coat striped with bright colors, which his father had given him, because he was a kind and obedient son, and could always be trusted.

Once he told his father of some wicked thing his brothers had done, and they hated him for it, and could not speak pleasantly to him.

MEETING OF JACOB AND ESAU.

Joseph had many strange and beautiful thoughts when he looked across the fields to the hills, and up into the starry sky at night. He also had some strange dreams that he told to his brothers. He said that he dreamed that they were binding sheaves in the field, and that his sheaf stood up, while the sheaves of his brothers bowed down to it.

Again he dreamed that the sun, and the moon, and eleven stars bowed down to him.

His father wondered that he should have such thoughts, and reproached him saying, "Shall I and thy brethren indeed come and bow down ourselves to thee to the earth?" and his brothers said,

"Shalt thou indeed rule over us?" and they hated him.

When they were many miles from home with the flocks their father sent Joseph to see if all was well with them. It was a long journey, and when they saw the boy coming they did not go to meet him, and speak kindly to him, but they said,

"Behold this dreamer is cometh. Let us slay him, and cast him into some pit, and we will say some evil beast hath devoured him, and we shall see what will become of his dreams."

But Reuben, the eldest, said,

"Let us not kill him; but cast him into this pit," hoping to take him out secretly, and send him to his father.

So when Joseph came near, they robbed him of his coat of many colors, and cruelly cast him into a pit. After this they sat down to eat their bread, and looking up they saw a caravan coming. It was a company of Ishmaelites carrying costly spices down into Egypt to sell them.

Then Judah said,

"Why should we kill our brother? Let us sell him to these Ishmaelites."

Then there passed by some Midianite merchants, and who drew Joseph out of the pit and sold him to the Ishmaelites for twenty pieces of silver, and he was carried down into Egypt.

Reuben, when his brothers went back to their flocks, went to the pit to try to save Joseph, but he was not there, and Reuben cried out,

"The child is not, and I, whither shall I go?"

The brothers who had been so cruel to Joseph brought his coat to their father, all stained with blood. They had themselves dipped it in the blood of a kid to deceive him, and he mourned long, and would not be comforted, for the beloved child that he believed had been torn in pieces by evil beasts.

CHAPTER VII.

JOSEPH, A SERVANT, A PRISONER, AND A SAINT.

The king of Egypt, where Joseph was taken by the Ishmaelites, was called Pharaoh, and he had a captain of the guard named Potiphar, who bought Joseph for a house servant. Though he was the son of a Hebrew prince, Joseph did his work faithfully and wisely as a servant, and was soon made steward of the house, and was trusted with all that his master had, and the Lord made all that he did to prosper; but the wife of Potiphar was a wicked woman, who persuaded her husband that Joseph was a bad man, and he was sent to prison.

Even there Joseph won the hearts of all, until the keeper of the prison set him over the other prisoners, and trusted him as Potiphar had done. It was the Lord in Joseph who helped him to win the love and trust of those around him.

Pharaoh sent two of his servants to prison because they had displeased him.

One was his chief cook, and one was the chief butler, who always handed the wine cup to the king, and Joseph had the care of them.

They each had a dream the same night, and were troubled because they could not understand them. Joseph asked them to tell him the dreams, for God knew what they meant.

So the chief butler told Joseph that he saw a vine having three branches, and the branches budded and blossomed, and the blossoms changed into ripe grapes, and he took the grapes and pressed them into Pharaoh's cup, and handed the cup to the king.

Then Joseph said: "The three branches are three days. Within three days the king will take you out of prison, and you shall hand the king's cup to him as you used to do."

Joseph also asked the butler, to think of him when he was again in the king's palace, and speak to the king to bring him out of prison, because he had been stolen from his own land, and he had done nothing wrong that he should be put in prison.

Then the chief cook told his dream. He said that he dreamed that he carried three baskets on his head, one above another.

In the highest one was all kinds of cooked meats for Pharaoh, and the birds flew down and ate from the basket.

"The three baskets are three days," said Joseph as he said to the butler, but he told the cook that in three days he would be put to death, and hanged on a tree, where the birds would eat his flesh.

All this came true, for Pharaoh's birthday came, and he brought out the chief butler to serve at a birthday feast, but he hanged the chief cook. Yet the chief butler forgot Joseph, and did not speak to the king about him as he might have done.

At the end of two long years, Pharaoh dreamed a dream. He thought he stood by the river of Egypt, and saw seven cows looking well kept and fat, came up out of the river.

Behind them came seven other cows, looking thin and poorly fed, and the thin and poorly fed cows ate up the well-kept and fat ones.

And Pharoah had a second dream. He thought he saw seven heads of wheat growing on one stalk—and they were all full of grain. After them came seven thin heads of wheat with no grain in them; and the seven bad heads of wheat ate up the seven good ones.

In the morning Pharaoh was troubled about these dreams, and called for his wise men who worked magic for him, and they could tell him nothing.

Then the chief butler standing near the king remembered Joseph, and told Pharaoh of the young Hebrew who had told the meaning of his dream, and that of the chief cook, and they had come to pass as he had said, so Pharaoh sent for Joseph and said to him:

"I have heard that thou canst understand a dream to interpret it."

Joseph answered the king humbly and wisely:

"It is not in me," he said, "God shall give Pharaoh an answer of peace."

When the king had told his dream Joseph said:

"The dream is one," and then he showed him that the seven fat cows, and the seven full heads of wheat meant seven good years in the land of Egypt, when the harvests would be great; and the seven lean cows, and the seven empty heads of wheat, meant seven years of famine, when the east winds should spoil the wheat, so there would be nothing to reap in time of harvest and the people would want bread. He told the king that he had better set a wise man over the land, who would attend to saving the grain during the seven good years, so that the people would have bread to eat in the seven years of famine.

JOSEPH SOLD INTO EGYPT.

The king was greatly pleased with Joseph, and told him that God had taught him to interpret dreams, and had showed him things to come, and there could be no wiser man found to be set over the land.

So he made Joseph a ruler over the whole land, and next to the king in all things.

He put his own ring on his hand, and dressed him in the robes of a prince, and gave him an Egyptian name and an Egyptian wife, so that there was no one in all the land of Egypt so great as Joseph, except the king.

He built storehouses in every city, and stored the grain, until it was like the sand of the sea, and could not be measured.

In the years of plenty two sons were born to Joseph, Manasseh and Ephraim, and then the seven years of dearth began to come. When the people began to cry to the king for bread, he always said,—

"Go to Joseph; what he says to you do."

And Joseph and his helpers began to open the storehouses, and sell wheat to the Egyptians, and to the people of all countries, for the famine was in all lands.

CHAPTER VIII.

JOSEPH—THE SAVIOR OF HIS PEOPLE.

The famine reached even to the fruitful land of Canaan, and Jacob, though rich in flocks and herds, began to need bread for his great family. So he sent his ten sons down into Egypt to buy wheat, keeping Benjamin, the youngest at home.

When they came before the governor they bowed down to him with their faces to the ground. Joseph knew them, though he acted as if he did not, and remembered his dream of his brother's sheaves bowing down to his sheaf. At first, he spoke roughly to them, and called them "spies." But they said that they were all one man's sons, and had come to buy food.

Joseph still spoke roughly to them, not because he was angry, but because he did not wish them to know him yet. His heart was full of love for them, and he was soon going to show them great kindness; but when they told him that they had left an old father and a young brother at home, and one was dead, he still acted as if they did not tell the truth.

He said that to prove themselves true men one of them should go home and bring the youngest brother, and the others should be kept in prison until they returned; and he put them all in prison.

After three days, he said one might stay while the others took the wheat home to their families, but that they must surely come back and bring the boy with them.

Then Reuben, who had tried to save Joseph from the pit long before, told his brothers that all this trouble had come upon them for their wickedness to their brother Joseph, and they said to each other in their own language:

"We are verily guilty concerning our brother; when he besought us, we would not hear, therefore is this distress come upon us."

Joseph understood everything they said though they did not know it, for he had been talking to them through an interpreter, and they thought he was an Egyptian. Now his heart was so full that he had to go out of the room to weep. But he came back and chose Simeon to stay while the others went to Canaan to bring back Benjamin.

They took the wheat that they had bought in bags, and went away; but when they stopped at an inn to rest and feed their asses, one of the brothers opened his bag, and found the money that he had paid for the wheat in the top of his bag. Here was more trouble, and they were afraid.

When they came home to their father they told him all that had happened, and as they opened the bags, each one found his money. Jacob was deeply troubled; for Joseph was gone, and Simeon was gone, and now they wanted to take Benjamin.

Reuben who had two sons said: "Slay my two sons if I bring him not to thee."

But Jacob said Benjamin should not go down to Egypt. But the wheat was gone in a short time, and they were likely to starve so great was the famine, and at last Jacob said they must go to Egypt again for food.

Judah said they would go if Benjamin would go with them, but Jacob would not listen to this. He asked them why they told the man that they had a brother, and they replied, that the Governor had asked them if their father was yet living and if they had another brother.

"Send the lad with me," said Judah, "if I bring him not unto thee, let me bear the blame forever."

Then Jacob told them to take him and go, and also to take presents of honey, and spices, and balm, and nuts, and double the money, so as to return that which was put in their bags, and he blessed them, and sent them away.

They went down into Egypt, and stood before Joseph again. When he saw Benjamin with them he told the steward of his house to make ready a fine dinner for them, and bring them to him at noon, and he did so.

Then the brothers were afraid that they were all to be put in prison, and at the door of Joseph's house began to tell the steward how they found the money when they opened their bags, and that they had brought it back doubled; but the steward spoke kindly to them, and said that he had placed their money, and that they need not fear, for God had given it back to them.

Then he brought Simeon out, and they made ready to dine with the Governor at noon, and to give him their presents.

When he came they bowed down to him and presented their gifts, and he asked them if they were well, and if the old man of whom they spoke was still alive, and they replied that he was. When he saw Benjamin, and knew that he was truly his own brother, the son of Rachel, he said:

"God be gracious unto thee my son," and he went quickly to his own chamber, lest he should weep before them.

When he came out to them again, and they sat down to dine, he placed the sons of Jacob by themselves, and the Egyptians of his house by themselves, and the brothers were placed according to their ages—Reuben at the head and Benjamin last, and they wondered among themselves at this. Joseph also sent portions from his own table to his brothers, but the portion of Benjamin was five times greater than that of the others.

The next morning their wheat was measured to them, and the asses were loaded with it, and they went on their way, but Joseph had told the steward to put the money of each man in the top of his bag, and in Benjamin's to put his silver cup.

When they were a little away from the city, the steward overtook them, and charged them with stealing his lord's silver cup.

The men were so sure that no one of them had stolen the silver cup, that they said,

"Let him die with whom the cup is found, and the rest of us will be your slaves."

So everybody's bag was opened from the oldest to the youngest, and the cup was found in Benjamin's bag. Then they rent their clothes for grief, and loaded the asses and went back to the city, and when they came to Joseph's

JOSEPH MAKES HIMSELF KNOWN TO HIS BROTHERS.

house, they fell on their faces before him. Joseph tried to speak sternly and said :

"What deed is this you have done?"

Judah said :

"What shall we say unto my lord, or how shall we clear ourselves? We are my lord's servants."

Then said Joseph :

"The man in whose hand the cup is found he shall be my servant, and as for you, get you up in peace unto your father."

Then Judah came nearer to Joseph, and all his soul came forth into his voice as he said :

"O, my lord, let thy servant speak a word in my lord's ears!"

Then he told the story of their coming down into Egypt, and of the old father and young brother whom he had asked them about; of the love of this father for the little one, for his mother, and his brother now dead. He reminded Joseph that he had told them to bring the boy to him, and that they had said, that if the boy should leave his father, his father would die ; but the governor had said, " Except your youngest brother come down with you, ye shall see my face no more."

Then Judah told the story of the father's grief when he found that he must let Benjamin go down into Egypt, that they might buy a little food ; how he spoke of his two sons, that were the sons of Rachel—that one had been torn in pieces, and now if mischief should befall the other, it would bring his gray hairs in sorrow to the grave. He asked Joseph what he should do when he returned to his father without the lad, seeing that his life was bound up in the lad's life, and Judah begged him, as he had made himself surety for the lad, to take him to be his slave, but to let Benjamin return to his father with his brothers.

"For how shall I go up to my father," said Judah, " and the lad be not with me?"

Then Joseph could bear it no longer. He told all the Egyptians to go out of the room, and then weeping so that the Egyptians and the people in the king's house heard, he made himself known to his brothers.

"I am Joseph, your brother," he said, " whom you sold into Egypt," and he begged them to come near to him.

"Be not grieved nor angry with yourselves," he said, for he saw that they were terrified, "for God sent me before you to save your lives by a great deliverance. It was not you that sent me hither, but God, and he hath made me a ruler throughout all the land of Egypt."

Then he told them to hasten and go to his father and tell him this, and ask him to come down at once, with all his flocks and herds, and dwell in Goshen, the best part of Egypt, for years of famine were yet to come.

Then Joseph took little Benjamin in his arms and wept over him, and kissed him, and kissed all his brothers, and after that his brothers talked with him. The king heard the story of Joseph's brothers and was pleased. He told Joseph to send wagons for the wives and little ones of his brothers, and to tell them to bring their father, and all their cattle and sheep, and come to live in Goshen where they should have the best of the land for their flocks and herds.

Joseph did as the king commanded, and also gave them food for the journey, and a suit of clothing to each brother, but to little Benjamin he gave five suits, and three hundred pieces of silver. He also loaded twenty asses with the good things of Egypt as presents to his father, so he sent them all on their journey saying:

"See that ye fall not out by the way."

When they came to Jacob in Hebron, they told him the wonderful story of the finding of Joseph, and his heart was faint, for he did not believe them; but when he had heard all Joseph's messages, and had seen the gifts, and the wagons, he said:

"It is enough: Joseph my son is yet alive: I will go and see him before I die."

So they began the long journey to Egypt, for it took a long time to travel with a great family, and with thousands of cattle and sheep. At Beersheba Jacob stopped and worshiped God, where his father had built an altar years before; and God told him in the night that he need not fear to go down into Egypt, for He would there make him a great nation, and that He would bring him back again to his own land.

So Jacob with all his children and their little ones, and all his flocks and herds came into Egypt. There were sixty-seven souls, and when they had counted Joseph and his two sons, there were seventy.

Jacob sent Judah on before to see Joseph and ask the way to Goshen, so that they might go directly there with the cattle and sheep. And when Joseph knew that his father was coming, he went to meet him in Goshen, and there he wept on his father's neck a long time, and Jacob said:

"Now let me die, since I have seen thy face, because thou art yet alive."

After this Joseph presented five of his brothers to Pharaoh, and the king spoke very kindly to them, and gave them the best of the land for their flocks, and hired some of them to oversee his own shepherds.

Joseph brought his father in also and Jacob blessed Pharaoh.

So the family of Jacob lived in peace, and were cared for by Joseph, just as the Lord had promised Jacob, when in a dream he saw the angels of God at Bethel, and heard above them the voice of the Lord blessing him, and saying:

"Thou shalt spread abroad to the West, and to the East, and to the North, and to the South, and in thee shall all the families of the earth be blessed."

Joseph carried all Egypt through the years of famine, and saved seed for the people to sow their fields in the seventh year so that they said:

"Thou hast saved our lives."

He afterwards visited his father, and Jacob made him promise that he would bury him when he died in the tomb of Abraham and Isaac, his father, in his own land.

When Jacob was near his end, Joseph brought his two little sons, Ephraim and Manasseh, to his bedside, and the old man gave them his blessing, laying his right hand upon the head of Ephraim, the youngest, and his left hand on that of Manasseh the first born, even as Isaac had given the birthright blessing to him instead of to Esau, and he said:

"The angel which redeemed me from all evil bless the lads."

Then he called all his sons together and told them what should befall them in the last days. To each one he spoke as a prophet speaks who has a vision of things to come, and he blessed them there. When he spoke to Judah, he told him that kings and lawgivers should arise from among his children until the Saviour of the world should come.

Jacob was an hundred and forty-seven years old when he died, and there was great mourning for him.

Joseph had the body of his father embalmed, as the Egyptians had the custom of doing, and after a long mourning in Egypt, Joseph and his brothers and many Egyptians who were Joseph's friends, carried the body of Jacob to Canaan, in a great procession, and buried him in the cave of Machpelah, where his fathers were buried.

After they had returned to Egypt, the brothers of Joseph said:

"Perhaps now he will hate us, and bring upon us all the evil we did to him."

So they sent to him to ask his forgiveness for all that was past. Then Joseph wept, for he had nothing but love in his heart toward his brothers, and he wished them to trust him. He comforted them and spoke kindly to them, saying:

"Fear not: ye meant evil unto me, but God meant it unto good. I will nourish you and your little ones."

And so through all Joseph's life, and he lived one hundred and ten years, he was a tender father to all his family, and a wise ruler of the people, and he died after making his family promise to carry his body back into Canaan to be buried with his fathers when they themselves should go.

"For God will surely visit you," he said, "and bring you out of this land into the land which he promised to Abraham, to Isaac and to Jacob."

CHAPTER IX.

THE CRADLE THAT WAS ROCKED BY A RIVER.

After Joseph and all the sons of Jacob had grown old and had passed away, their children's children grew in numbers until they became a great multitude.

The Pharaoh whom Joseph had served also died, and the king who followed him did not like the Hebrews. He feared them because they had grown to be strong, so he set overseers to watch them, and make them work like slaves.

He treated them cruelly, and made them lift the great stones with which they built the tombs of the kings and temples of the gods. He also tried to kill all the little boys as soon as they were born, but the Lord took care of them. Also, the king told his servants, that wherever they found a baby boy among the Hebrews, to throw him into the river Nile, but the little girls, they should save alive.

There was a man named Amrom, who, with his wife Jochebed, had a beautiful little boy whom they tenderly loved. They hid him as long as they could, and then when he was three months old and she could hide him no longer, she made up her mind to give him into the care of God. She made a little boat, or ark of stout rushes, that grew by the river. She wove it closer than a basket, and then covered it with pitch that the water might not enter, just as Noah covered the great ark before the flood.

Then she wrapped her baby carefully and laid him in the little boat, and set it among the reeds at the edge of the river Nile. God and His angels watched the cradle of the child, and the river gently rocked it. Jochebed told the baby's sister to wait near by and see what might happen to him, and this is what happened, or rather what God prepared for the baby in the boat of rushes.

The king's daughter came down to bathe in the river, and as her maidens walked up and down by the riverside, she called one of them to bring to her the little ark that she saw rocking on the river among the reeds. When she had opened it she saw a beautiful little child, and when it cried her heart was touched, and she longed to keep it for her own.

"This is one of the Hebrew's children," she said, and as the baby's sister came near she asked the princess if she should go and get a nurse from among the Hebrew women to bring it up for her, and the princess said to her, "Go," and the maid went and called the child's mother. The princess said: "Take this child away and nurse it for me, and I will give thee thy wages."

And the mother took her baby joyfully though she hid her joy in her heart, and carried him home to nurse and bring up for Pharoah's daughter.

And the child grew, and when he was old enough his mother took him to the king's palace, and he became the son of the princess. She called his name Moses, which means "drawn out," because she drew him out of the water.

THE FINDING OF MOSES.

CHAPTER X.

MOSES IN MIDIAN.

Moses had teachers, and was taught all the learning of the Egyptians, but his heart was with his own people. He was grieved when he saw their burdens, and heard their cries when their taskmasters struck them.

Once, when he was a grown man, he saw an Egyptian beating a Hebrew, and he struck the Egyptian and killed him, for he thought he ought to defend his people: and when he saw that the man was dead, he buried him in the sand. In a day or two Moses tried to make peace between two Hebrews who were fighting, and they answered him roughly, and one of them said:

"Who made thee a ruler over us? wilt thou kill me, as thou didst the Egyptian yesterday?"

Then Moses was afraid, and when the king heard of it, and tried to take his life, Moses fled away out of Egypt, through a desert into Midian. There he found a well and sat down by it to rest. While he sat there the seven daughters of the priest of Midian came to draw water for their father's flocks, and some rough shepherds came and drove them away, but Moses stood up and helped them, and watered their flocks. When their father knew that a noble stranger had been kind to his daughters, he asked him to come into his house, and eat bread with him, and stay as long as he would. So Moses stayed and Zipporah, one of the seven sisters, became his wife.

But Moses did not forget his people. God was preparing him to lead them out of bondage, and he learned many things, during the years that he kept the sheep of his father-in-law in the wilderness.

One day he led his flocks across the desert to Mount Horeb or Sinai. There he saw a bush all bright within as if it burned. He drew nearer to see why the bush was not consumed, and heard the voice of the Lord calling him. The Lord told him to come no nearer, and to put off his shoes, for he stood on holy ground. Then the Lord told him that He was the God of his fathers, and that He had heard the cry of his oppressed people in Egypt.

"I know their sorrows," said the voice from the midst of the fire, "And I am come down to deliver them out of the hand of the Egyptians, and to bring them up out of that land into a good land, and a large—unto a land flowing with milk and honey."

Then the Lord said that Moses must go to the new Pharaoh, for the old king was dead, and bring the children of Israel out of Egypt. Moses was a very humble man, and he could not believe that Pharaoh would listen to him, or that the Hebrews would follow him, but the Lord said,

"Certainly I will be with thee."

And as a sign that it should be so, He said that after Moses had brought his people out of Egypt, they should serve God in this mountain.

But Moses had many fears. He knew that he had been brought up as an Egyptian, and he feared that his people would not listen to his words.

Then the Lord showed signs to Moses to help his faith.

He turned the rod in Moses' hand into a serpent, and then when he was afraid of it, the Lord told him to take it in his hand and it became a rod again.

He also turned his hand white with leprosy, and then changed it again to natural flesh, and told Moses, that these, and other signs he should show in Egypt—to prove that he was sent of God.

But Moses felt himself to be so weak and faithless as a leader of his people, that he still cried out that he was "slow of speech, and of a slow tongue," and when the Lord said, "I will teach thee what thou shalt say," he did not believe, but begged the Lord to send by whom he would, only not by him.

Then the Lord said that Aaron, the brother of Moses could speak well, and that he should go with him to Pharoah and to his people, and should speak for him, but that the wisdom and power of God should be with Moses, and that he should do wonders with the rod in his hand.

CHAPTER XI.

THE ROD THAT TROUBLED EGYPT.

So Moses took his wife and his sons and returned to Egypt, and the rod of God was in his hand; and Aaron, sent of God, came to meet him in the wilderness, and there Moses told him all that was in his heart, and all that God had sent him to do.

When they came into Egypt they gathered the Israelites together, and Aaron spoke to them, and they believed his words, and the signs that Moses showed them.

Afterward, they went to Pharoah and gave him the message of the Lord, and Pharoah said:

"I know not the Lord, neither will I let Israel go."

And he began to oppress the Israelites more than he had ever done before. They made bricks of clay mixed with straw, that hardened in the sun, and were as lasting as stone, but he forced them to find the straw wherever they could, and make as many bricks as before. This they did until no more straw could be found, and their Egyptian masters beat them cruelly because they failed to make the full number of bricks. Then they turned upon Moses and Aaron and said, that they had put a sword in the kings hand to slay them.

Where could Moses turn except to the Lord who had sent him? The Lord heard him and made to him again the great promise, as he did at the burning bush, and Moses told the people, but they could not believe it, for they were crushed under their cruel burdens.

And now the Lord sent Moses and Aaron again to Pharoah, to show by sign and miracle, that their message was from Him. They took the rod that Moses brought from Mount Horeb, and Moses told Aaron to cast it down before the king, and it became a serpent. Pharoah called his wise men and wizards, and they did the same, only Aaron's rod swallowed up their rods, and Pharoah would not listen to their words.

But in the morning when Pharoah walked by the river the two men stood by him and said again:

The Lord God of the Hebrews hath sent me unto thee saying:

"Let my people go that they may serve me in the wilderness," and then Aaron struck the waters of the river Nile with his rod, and the waters turned to blood.

In all the land, in every stream and pond there was blood, so that the fishes died and no one could drink the water.

But because the wizards could turn water to blood also, Pharoah's heart was hardened toward Moses and Aaron.

While the people were digging wells for water, Aaron stretched forth his rod over the river again, and frogs came up from it, and spread over all the land and filled the houses of the people. This also the magicians did, but so great was the plague that the king said:

"I will let the people go."

"When shall I entreat for thee and for thy people to destroy the frogs from thee and thy houses?" said Moses; and Pharoah told him to do so the next day.

THE ROD THAT TROUBLED EGYPT.

So on the next day Moses prayed to the Lord that the frogs might go out of the land, and the Lord answered his prayer; but when Pharoah saw that the frogs had been destroyed his heart grew hard, and he would not listen to Moses and Aaron.

Then another plague was brought upon the Egyptians. The dust of the land was changed to lice that covered man and beast, and this was followed by swarms of flies that settled upon all the land except Goshen where the Israelites lived.

Then Pharoah said:

"Go, sacrifice to your God in this land," but they would not worship in Egypt, and Pharoah at last told them that they could go into the wilderness, but they must not go very far away. So Moses prayed, and the swarms of flies were swept out of Egypt, but Pharoah did not keep his word.

Then a great sickness fell upon the cattle and sheep of the country, though the flocks and herds of the Israelites were free from it; and this was followed by a breaking out of boils upon men and beasts everywhere, even upon the magicians, but Pharoah's heart was still too wicked to yield to God.

Then came a great storm of hail over Egypt, such as had never been known in that sunny land. It killed the cattle in the fields, and destroyed the grain that was grown, and broke the trees and herbs. The lightnings fell also and ran upon the ground, and when it was over the heart of Pharoah was still hard against God.

Then Moses told Pharoah that the face of the earth would be covered with clouds of locusts that would eat every green thing left by the storm, if he did not let God's people go. This frightened Pharoah's servants and they begged him to send them away, and though he would not let their wives and little ones go, he said:

"Go now, ye that are men, for that ye did desire," and he drove them out of his presence.

Then at the Lord's word, Moses arose and stretched forth his rod over Egypt, and the plague of locusts came, driven by the East wind, and covered the land until there was no green thing left in Egypt.

Then Pharaoh sent for Moses and Aaron in great haste, and confessing his sin, begged to be forgiven and to be saved from, "this death only," and, at Moses' prayer, a mighty west wind drove the army of locusts into the Red Sea.

But again the heart of Pharaoh turned against God, and the Lord brought thick darkness over the land for three days, only in the homes of the Hebrews there was light. Then Pharaoh was willing to let them take their wives and their little ones, but not their flocks and herds, and because they would not leave them behind, Pharaoh drove Moses and Aaron from him in anger, saying:

"See my face no more."

But the Lord proposed to break the hard heart of Pharaoh. He told Moses to see that every Israelite should take a lamb from the flock and keep it four days. Then, at evening, he was to kill it, and dip a branch of hyssop in its blood, and strike it against the sides of his door, also over it, leaving three marks of blood there. Then he was to close his door and no one was to go out of it until morning.

They were to roast the lamb and eat of it, and be ready for the journey they were to make, and it should be to them forever the feast called the Passover. They were to eat it with unleavened bread, and the feast should be kept forever from the first to the seventh day of the month, a holy feast to the Lord.

And this is why it was called the feast of the Passover. At midnight, after the lamb was killed in each house of the Israelites, and the doors were shut, the Lord passed through the land, and wherever he saw the blood on the side posts and the top of the door, he passed over that house, and it was safe, but in every Egyptian house the first born died, from the child of Pharaoh who sat on the throne, to the child of the captive in the cell, and all the first born of cattle.

The next morning a great cry went up from the land of Egypt, for there was not a house where there was not one dead.

Then Pharaoh was quite ready to let the Israelites go.

"Take all you have and be gone," he said.

They were all ready, and rose up very gladly to join the great procession, led by Moses and Aaron, that gathered in Goshen, and started on its long journey toward the east.

They had heard of the land of their fathers, and now they were going home to be slaves no more. They were a family of seventy souls when they came into Egypt, four hundred and thirty years before, and now they went out a great nation, as the Lord had promised when he blessed their fathers.

The feast of the Passover has been the chief one held by the Israelites, from the time of their coming out of Egypt until now, and since Jesus held the Passover feast with his disciples on the night that he went forth to death, it has become to all Christians the Sacrament of the Lord's Supper.

CHAPTER XII.

FOLLOWING THE CLOUD.

"God led the people," says the Word, as they came up out of Egypt. He gave them the two leaders by whom He had broken the power of Pharaoh, and set His people free, and He also set a great cloud in the air, just above and before them, to lead them in the right way. It was to them the presence of the Lord. By day it rose white and beautiful against the blue sky, and moved slowly before them. At night it stood still while they rested, and shed light over all the camp, for there seemed to be a fire within the cloud at night. How safe and happy they must have felt away from the cruel taskmasters of Egypt, and the Lord's presence, spreading a wing of cloud over them. They were not led by a straight way to Canaan, for a warlike people lived in the land which they must pass through, but they were led at first through a country without cities or armies, where they would not trouble many people or be troubled by them. They bore with them the embalmed body of Joseph, for they had promised to bury him with his fathers in the cave of Machpelah; and they also had much wealth in herds, and flocks, and gold, and silver. Pharaoh thought of this after they had gone, and his wicked heart grew harder than before, so he ordered his chariots and horsemen to follow them, and they found the Israelites camped by the Red Sea.

Then there was great fear and mourning in the camp when they saw the army of Pharaoh coming, but Moses cried:

"Fear ye not, stand still and see the salvation of the Lord. The Lord shall fight for you, and ye shall hold your peace."

Then the Lord told Moses to speak to the people that they go forward. He also told him to lift up his rod and stretch his hand over the sea and divide it, and the children of Israel should go on dry ground through the midst of the sea. Night was falling, and the waters lay dark before them, but the angel of God, the pillar of cloud and fire, moved from its place before them and went behind them, while Moses and Aaron led them on. Then the presence of the Lord was a cloud and darkness to the Egyptians, but it gave a light by night to the Israelites. A strong east wind drove the waters apart all night, so that there was a way through the sea, and the waters were a wall upon their right hand and on their left. Pharaoh's army saw the broad path

DESTRUCTION OF PHAROAH'S ARMY.

through the sea, and followed fast after the Israelites, but as morning dawned the Lord looked from the cloud and troubled the Egyptians. Their chariot wheels came off, and all went wrong with them.

At last the Lord told Moses to stretch his hand forth over the sea, that the waters might come back upon the Egyptians, and he did so; and as the sun rose, the sea swallowed up the Egyptian host, and their bodies were cast upon the shore. There on the other side stood the great host of Israel, and saw the salvation of God, and they believed in Him, and in Moses His servant.

Then a great shout went up from the host of Israel. Moses led them in a song of praise, and Miriam, the sister of Aaron, took a tambourine, and the women followed her in dances as they answered in a chorus of praise:—

"Sing ye to the Lord, for He hath triumphed gloriously; the horse and the rider hath he thrown into the sea."

Soon they took up their journey, the cloudy pillar going before. There was but little water by the way, and after three days of thirst, they came to the waters of Marah, but they were bitter, and the people cried to Moses,

"What shall we drink?"

Then the Lord showed him a tree which he cast into the waters, and they were made pure and sweet. Soon after they came to Elim, where there were twelve wells of water, and seventy palm trees, and there they rested.

Again they took up their journey and passed through a desert land, where they could get no food, and again they complained to Moses because he had brought them into the wilderness to die. They did not yet believe that God could supply all their need.

"I will rain bread from heaven for you," said the Lord to Moses. He was ready to provide, if they would only believe in Him and obey Him.

Moses called them to come near before the Lord while Aaron should speak his word to them. As they came near and looked toward the wilderness where the cloud stood, the glory of the Lord shone out of it. The Lord had heard them speak harshly to Moses for bringing them into a desert to die, but he said,

"At even ye shall eat flesh, and in the morning ye shall be filled with bread."

And his word came true. Great flocks of quails came up and covered the camp at sunset, so that they caught them for food; and in the morning the dew lay around them, and when it had risen, there lay on the ground a small, round, white thing, something like frost, or a little seed, and it tasted like wafers made with honey. The Lord told Moses that the people must gather just enough to eat through the day, and no more. The morning before the Sabbath they must gather enough for two days, for none would fall on the Sabbath. This was the bread that the heavenly Father provided for his children through all the years of their journey from Egypt to Canaan, and they called it "Manna."

There were hard things to bear in the wilderness. Often when they wanted water for their little ones and their cattle, and could not find it, they were like fretful children when they were tired and thirsty. Once, at Horeb, Moses struck a rock with his wonderful rod, and water sprung out in a stream.

There were enemies also in the way. The Amelikites came out to fight with the Israelites. The strong men went to meet the enemy, but Moses stood on a hill with the rod of God in his hand, and Aaron and Hur were with him. While Moses held up the rod, Israel prevailed; but when he let down his hand Amalek prevailed.

But Moses grew tired and they placed a stone for him to sit upon, and Aaron and Hur held up his hands on either side until the going down of the sun, when Amalek was conquered. Moses built an altar there, and called it "The Lord my Banner."

They were now drawing near the Mount, where Moses saw the burning bush, and heard the Lord calling him to be the leader of his people.

They were far out of their way to Canaan, but it was in the Lord's purpose to bring them into obedience and faith before he brought them into the promised land. They had lived long among the Egyptians, and were very far from being like Jacob and Joseph, but there were good and true men like Aaron, and Joshua, and Hur, who helped Moses. It was about three months after the children of Israel left Egypt, that they came into the wilderness of Sinai. There the "Mount of God" still lifts its great granite cliffs toward the sky. There are high valleys midway where it is cooler than below, and there the people encamped and waited to hear what God would say to them, for God talked with Moses on the Mount.

He said He had chosen them, if they would obey his voice, to be a holy nation. He told Moses to tell the people to be ready, and on the third day He would come down in the sight of all the people on Mount Sinai.

And so it was, as the people looked there was a thick cloud upon the Mount, from which came thunder and lightning, and the sound of a great trumpet, while the mountain trembled as with an earthquake. Only Moses and Aaron could approach the holy Mount, and from it God gave to Moses the laws that the people were to live by, and Moses wrote them all down that he might read them to the people. A company of the Elders of Israel went up and saw the glory of God afar off, but God called Moses up into the Mount, and the cloud closed him round, while the Lord gave him the laws for a great nation, and the pattern of the tabernacle which He wished him to make for a church in the wilderness.

Forty days and forty nights Moses was on the Mount with God, and then God gave him the ten great commandments written with his own hands on tablets of stone, that he might give them to the people. They were to be kept as the rules of life for all people in all times.

Forty days and nights seemed a long time to the people camped around the Mount. Perhaps they thought Moses would never come back to lead them, for they began to think of the gods of Egypt, and asked Aaron to make one for them. So to please them he told them to bring him their gold ornaments, and he melted them and made a golden calf such as the Egyptians worshiped, and before it they made an altar, and they worshiped the calf.

The Lord who sees all things told Moses to go down to the people for they were worshiping an idol. So Moses went down a little way and met Joshua, and they both went down and saw the people feasting, and singing, and dancing, and Moses cast the tablets of stone upon the ground and they were broken. The heart of Moses, too, was almost broken, but he destroyed the golden calf, and punished the people for their great sin, and then went up to the Mount to plead for the life of his people.

"O this people have sinned a great sin," he cried, "and have made them gods of gold, yet now if thou wilt forgive their sin, and if not, blot me, I pray thee, out of the book which thou has written," so great was the love of Moses for his people.

There was a time of repentance among the people after this, and Moses and his servant Joshua reared a tent outside the camp and called it the Tabernacle of the congregation. It was for worship until the true Tabernacle should be built according to the pattern given in the Mount. All who sought the Lord went to worship there, and the pillar of cloud came and stood at the Tabernacle door while Moses talked with God, and all the people saw it and worshiped.

Moses prayed again for the people, and the Lord said:

"My presences shall go with thee, and I will give thee rest."

The Lord called Moses again into the mount, and told him to bring with

MOSES DESCENDING FROM THE MOUNT.

him two tablets of stone and He would again write the ten commandments upon them.

So Moses hewed them from the rock and took them up into Mount Sinai. Then the Lord came down again in a thick cloud and talked with Moses, and wrote upon the tablets of stone.

After forty days Moses came down to the people bringing the commandments with him, but his face shone with a strange light that the people never saw before, and they were afraid of him. It was something above the light of the sun, for Moses had seen the Glory of the Lord.

While they still camped around the mount they began to build the Tabernacle. Moses told the people to bring gold, and silver, and brass, and wood. They also brought precious stones, and oil for the lamp, and fine linen, and they gave so willingly that at last Moses told them that there was more than enough.

These were put in the hands of two wise men whom the Lord had chosen and taught to do the work, and they had willing helpers among the people, for wise hearted women did spin with their own hands, and bring what they had spun, of blue, and purple, and scarlet, and fine linen to make the hangings of the Tabernacle.

If you would know all the beautiful and costly and curious things that were made for this church in the wilderness, you will find them described in the last chapters of Exodus.

The Israelites camped a long time in the high valleys around the Mount of God, and at last set up the Tabernacle. It was so made that it could be taken down and carried with them when they journeyed, for it was a beautiful tent. Over it the pillar of cloud stood. Whenever it moved the people followed, and when it stood still, they rested. Within the Tabernacle they placed a beautiful chest of wood overlaid with gold, which ever after held their most precious things, the tablets of stone written upon by the Lord himself.

This "Ark of Testimony," as it was called, had rings at the sides through which men laid strong rods by which to carry it, and so had the golden table for bread, and the golden altar of incense. There was a beautiful seven-branched candlestick of pure gold in which olive oil was burned for a sacred sign, and there was a brazen altar for burnt offerings, and a great brazen bowl for washing, and other things to be used in the worship of the Sanctuary.

There were beautiful garments, also, for the priests, Aaron and his sons, and for Aaron there was a wonderful breast-plate of gold set with twelve precious stones, bearing the names of the twelve tribes of Israel.

When all was finished, and the Tabernacle was set up, the cloud that veiled the presence of the Lord came and covered it, and the glory of the Lord filled it, so that Moses could not enter; but the Lord spoke to him from the cloud, and told him how the priests should order the worship of the Lord there.

Afterward, Aaron and his sons offered burnt offerings for their sins, and the sins of the people, in the way the Lord had commanded, and fire from the Lord came down and consumed the offering.

When the people saw the answer of the Lord they fell on their faces before him.

In the second month of the second year the cloud rose from over the Tabernacle, and then the people knew it was time to go on their journey. So they took down the tent of the Tabernacle and put all things in order for the journey. Each of the twelve tribes descended from the twelve sons of Jacob marched by themselves, carrying banners, and having captains. In the midst of them all marched the Levites carrying the Ark and the different parts of the Tabernacle, and when the cloud stood still, they stopped and set up the Tabernacle, while the people formed their camp all around it in the order of their tribes.

Still the manna fell with the dew at night, and the people gathered it in the morning, and when they tired of it, the Lord sent them quails again.

Over and over the people complained and rebelled, but the Angel of the Lord's Presence still hovered over them, and led them toward the promised land. Forty years they were on the journey that was so easily made by the sons of Jacob when they went back and forth to buy wheat in the time of famine; and forty-two times did they encamp on the way, yet the mercy of the Lord never failed them, and they were brought into their own land at last. Then the cloud was no longer needed to go before them, but long after, when they built a beautiful temple at Jerusalem in which to put the sacred Ark of Testimony, the cloud came again and filled the temple with the glory of the Lord.

CHAPTER XIII.

IN THE BORDERS OF CANAAN.

While the host of Israel was in camp at Paran, the Lord told Moses to send men before them into Canaan to spy out the land.

So he sent twelve men who walked through the land and saw the people, and the cities and the fields and the fruits. They were forty days searching the land and they brought from the brook Eschol a cluster of grapes so large that two of them bore it on a staff between them. They also brought some pomegranates and figs.

When they came into the camp they said that the country where they had been was good, and flowing with milk and honey, but the people were strong, and the cities had very high walls. They said they saw giants there.

Caleb, who was one of the twelve, and a good and true man, said:

"Let us go up at once and possess it, for we are well able to overcome it," but the men who were with him were afraid of the giants, and said they felt like grasshoppers before them. Then there was great weeping among the people all that night, and they said,

"Let us make a captain, and let us return into Egypt." Moses and Aaron were greatly troubled, but the two good men, Caleb and Joshua, stood up and encouraged the people, saying that they need not fear, for the Lord had given them the land, yet they were ready to stone Caleb and Joshua.

Then the Lord spake to Moses from the Tabernacle, and the people saw his glory. He said the people were unbelieving and disobedient, and for this reason they could not enter the promised land. He said, that all who were twenty years old and upward would die in the wilderness, except Caleb and Joshua, who had followed the Lord wholly. He also said that the people would be forty years in the wilderness, and only the youth and the children would live to enter Canaan.

There was mourning and repentance then because of the word of the Lord, and the people promised again to believe and obey, but over and over they lost faith and rebelled, and great storms of trouble fell upon them.

Once the earth opened and many were swallowed up; a sudden sickness destroyed thousands. Near Mount Hor, where Aaron died, fiery serpents ran among the people, and all who were bitten by them died; but there was

THE RETURN OF THE SPIES.

full forgiveness and cure for those who turned to the Lord. When the fiery serpents entered the camp Moses lifted a brazen image of a serpent up on a pole so high that it could be seen all over the camp, and whoever looked upon it lived. It was a sign of the coming Saviour.

Between the marches and the battles with heathen tribes, some of whom were giants, Moses wrote in a book the laws that God gave him for the government of the people. They were wise laws, the keeping of which would bring health, peace and blessedness to the people. He gave the book to the Levites who carried the Ark, and they were to keep it always beside the Ark, and often read it aloud to the people.

Moses said many things to the people, and as Jacob blessed his twelve sons, so Moses blessed each of the twelve tribes that descended from them, for he was near the end of his long life. The Lord had told him that He should take him to Himself before the people entered Canaan, and that Joshua must lead the people into the promised land. So when they had reached the borders of Canaan, and were encamped near the Jordan, the Lord called his tried servant up into Mount Nebo, that he might see the land beyond the Jordan, where the twelve tribes were to find their promised home. Then the Lord gave him a view of the land, and there he died, as Aaron died on Mount Hor.

No one saw Moses die, and no one knows where he was buried, for the Lord buried him. He was one hundred and twenty years old, and yet as strong as a young man. After his death Joshua became the leader of Israel.

CHAPTER XIV.

A NATION THAT WAS BORN IN A DAY.

The time had come for the people to cross the river Jordan, and enter their own land, and the Lord told Joshua to prepare the people for their last journey before going over Jordan. Joshua first sent two men over the river to see the land.

They went to the walled city of Jericho, and to the house of a woman named Rahab. The king heard that they were there and sent for them, but the woman hid them under the flax that she was drying on the roof of her

CROSSING THE JORDAN.

house. Afterward she let them down by a rope through a window (for her house was built on the town wall), and they escaped. They promised Rahab before they went, that if she would hang a long line of scarlet thread from the window on the wall, that when they came to take the city she should be saved and all her family because of her kindness to them.

After they had returned to the camp they told Joshua that the Lord would surely give them the land, for the people were afraid of them. Then they rose up and marched to the banks of the Jordan and waited for Joshua to lead them over. Some of them remembered how they had passed through the Red Sea, and others had heard it from their parents, and they now waited to see the salvation of God. Joshua told them to follow the priests, and the Levites who would bear the Ark of the Covenant, so when Joshua said:

"Behold the Ark of the Covenant of the Lord of all the earth passeth over before you into Jordan," the people followed.

The Jordan lay spread before them like a lake, for it was the time of year when it overflowed all its banks, but when the feet of the priests who bore the Ark were dipped in the edge of the water, the waters from above stopped and rose like a wall, while the waters below flowed away into the Dead Sea, and left a wide path for the people to walk in, and the Ark stood still in Jordan until every one had passed over. Then twelve men, one out of every tribe, took a stone from the bed of the river and carried it over for a memorial altar, so that when any should ask in years to come, "What do these stones mean?" someone might tell them how the Lord led Israel through Jordan into their own land.

After the Ark had come up from the bed of Jordan, and there was not one of all the thousands of Israel left behind, the waters came down from the place where they had stayed, and flowed down into the Dead Sea, and overflowed the banks of Jordan as before.

The stones were heaped in Gilgal where they camped, and directly before them rose the walls of Jericho, and here they kept the passover. For forty years they had been fed with manna from heaven as they camped or journeyed in the wilderness, but now they began to eat the grain and the fruits of the land, and the manna fell no more.

Nearly five hundred years before the family of Jacob left this land to go down into Egypt where Joseph was. They grew to be a great people, but they were slaves. Then the Lord sent Moses to make them free, and they began the long journey, which at last brought them to their own land.

Forty years they were on the journey, and all this time they were pilgrims, but on the day that the Jordan ceased to flow, and parted while they passed over into the land promised to their fathers, they became a nation.

The land was before them, and they had only to obey the Lord and his servant Joshua to conquer and possess it.

As they filled the valley of the Jordan before Jericho, the hearts of the heathen fainted for fear, for they knew that only the Lord could divide a river to let his people pass.

Joshua went out of the camp to look at Jericho, the walled city. It was shut up for fear of the Israelites, and there was no one to be seen.

Suddenly Joshua saw a warrior standing with a drawn sword in his hand.

"Art thou for us," said Joshua, "or for our adversaries?" and the warrior angel answered,

"Nay! but as Captain of the host of the Lord, am I now come," and Joshua fell on his face before him.

He knew then that it was the Lord who would conquer Jericho, and he was told how the people were to help him.

So Joshua called the priests, and told them to take up the Ark, and he told seven priests to go before it bearing trumpets of rams' horns. Then the army of Israel, ready for war, followed, half of them marching before the Ark, and half of them coming after, and as the trumpets gave a great sound, they marched once around the city, and then went to camp. This they did once every day for seven days, but on the seventh day they marched around the city seven times, and as the priests blew the trumpets for the last time, Joshua cried with a mighty voice,

"Shout! for the Lord hath given you the city."

Then as a great shout went up from the people, the walls of the city fell down flat, so that the soldiers of Israel went up, every man straight before him, and took Jericho.

And Rahab was not forgotten. The Lord cared for her little house on the wall, and she, with all her family, were brought into the Camp of Israel.

And so by the conquest of Jericho the new nation of Israel began to possess its land.

CHAPTER XVI.

SAMSON THE STRONG.

All the days of Joshua—and he lived to be an hundred and ten years old—the Israelites were conquering the people who lived in Canaan, and dividing it among the tribes. Joshua was a father to them, as Moses had been, and when at last they were at rest, each tribe within its own borders, and they had begun to build their houses, and plant their fields, Joshua spoke words of loving counsel to the people, and they set up a stone under an oak tree, as a sign that they would always serve the Lord and keep the law, and then he went to be with God. After his death Israel was ruled by wise men called judges, who helped them to conquer the land little by little. Some of them were good men and brave warriors as Othniel and Gideon and Jephthah, and one was a prophetess named Deborah, a noble mother in Israel, and one was a mighty man of strength, Samson, the son of Manoah.

The people of Israel had turned away from the Lord, and could no longer conquer their enemies, but the Philistines had conquered them, and had been their masters for forty years, when the Lord sent Samson to deliver them. He was not a wise man like Moses or Joshua, but he had great strength, and the Lord used him against the Philistines.

Once a young lion came roaring against him, and he caught it and rent it in two, as if it had been a kid. When he passed the same way afterward he saw that the bees had built a nest in the body of the lion, and it was full of honey. At his marriage feast—for he married a Philistine woman—he made a riddle for the young men to guess:

"Out of the eater came forth meat, and out of the strong, come forth sweetness."

They tried for seven days to guess the riddle, but they could not, and then they told Samson's wife to find it out for them, or they would burn her house. She begged him with tears to tell her, and at last he told her of the honey comb in the body of the lion, and she told the young men, so that at the end of the seventh day they said to Samson,

"What is sweeter than honey?" and "what is stronger than a lion?"

He saw that he had been betrayed, so he paid his debt, a suit of clothes to each guest, and went home to his father's house. Afterwards when he

THE YOUNG SAMSON.

found that his wife had been given to another he tied firebrands to the tails of three hundred foxes, and sent them among the wheat fields of the Philistines so that the fields were set on fire.

Once the men of Gaza tried to kill him when he was within their city, but he rose at midnight and took the city gates, with its posts and bar, and carried them away on his shoulders to the top of the hill. Again the Philistine lords had promised a great deal of money to a woman, if she would get Samson to tell her what made him so strong, so she begged him to tell her. Three times she thought she knew the secret, and told the Philistines, but they could not bind him. At last he was tired of her questions, and said to her plainly—that from a child no razor had ever touched his hair. If it should be cut he would be as weak as other men. Then she watched and cut his hair while he slept, and the Philistines bound him and carried him to Gaza, where they made him blind, and forced him to grind in the mills of a prison house. The Philistines were glad because Samson was their prisoner at last, and so they came together in a great feast to sacrifice to their god Dagon, for they said,

"Our god has delivered Samson into our hands." While they were merry they said:

"Let us send for Samson to make sport for us," and he was brought out of the prison. It was very sad to see the strong judge of Israel, weak and blind, led by a little lad, and making sport for the people in front of their temple. All the lords of the Philistines were there, and upon the broad roof of the temple were about three thousand people watching Samson while he showed his strength, for his hair had grown and his strength was returning. At last as he was standing between two great pillars that held up the roof, he prayed, lifting his sightless eyes to God:

"O Lord God, remember me, I pray thee, and strengthen me only this once."

Then he clasped his arms around the pillars on either side of him, and bowing himself with all his might, saying,

"Let me die with the Philistines," he drew the great pillars with him, and the house fell with all that were upon it, on all that were within it. So died Samson who judged Israel twenty years, yet a woman, Deborah, who was also one of the judges in Israel, was stronger than he, for the Lord looketh on the heart.

THE DEATH OF SAMSON.

CHAPTER XVII.

RUTH.

In the days when the judges ruled in Israel, there was a famine in the land, and an Israelite, who lived in Bethlehem, took his wife and his two sons into Moab where there was food. After a while the Israelite died, and the two sons married women of Moab.

After two years the sons died also, and their mother, Naomi, longed for her home in Bethlehem, for there was no longer a famine there. So she took Ruth and Orpah, her sons' wives, and started on the journey into the land of Israel.

But before they had gone far Naomi said:

"Go! return each to her mother's house; the Lord deal kindly with you, as ye have dealt with the dead, and with me."

She kissed them, and they wept and would not leave her.

"Turn again, my daughters," she said, "why will ye go with me?"

And Orpah kissed Naomi, and went back to her own mothers' house, but Ruth, whose heart was with Naomi, would not go back.

"Entreat me not to leave thee," she said, "or to return from following after thee, for where thou goest I will go; and where thou lodgest I will lodge; thy people shall be my people, and thy God my God; where thou diest I will die, and there will I be buried; the Lord do so to me, and more also, if aught but death part thee and me."

And so they came to Bethlehem, and the old friends of Naomi greeted her tenderly, and welcomed her back. It was about the beginning of the barley harvest.

There was a good and great man in Bethlehem named Boaz, and he was of the family of Naomi's husband. He had a field of barley where the reapers were at work, and Ruth asked Naomi if she should not go and glean after the reapers, to get grain, for they were poor.

Naomi said, "Go, my daughter," and she went.

When Boaz came out of the town into his field and greeted his reapers, he said to his servant having charge of the reapers,

"What maiden is this?" and he told him that she was the Moabitish girl who had come back with her mother-in-law Naomi.

RUTH GLEANING.

Then Boaz spoke very kindly to Ruth, and told her to stay with his maidens, and freely drink of the water drawn for them, and Ruth bowed before him and asked why he should be so kind to a stranger. He told her that he knew all her kindness to her mother-in-law since the death of her husband, and how she had left her own family and country to come among strangers, and he blessed her, saying,

"A full reward be given thee of the Lord God of Israel, under whose wings thou art come to trust."

Then he told her to sit down and eat bread with them, and he helped her to the parched corn with his own hands, and when they returned to work he told his young men to let her glean among the sheaves and reprove her not, and to let some handfuls fall purposely for her to glean. When Ruth went home Naomi said,

"Where hast thou gleaned to-day?" and Ruth told her. Then Naomi blessed Boaz, and told Ruth that he was one of their near relatives.

And so Ruth gleaned in the fields of Boaz through all the barley and the wheat harvest. When all the reaping was done, the grain was threshed on a piece of ground made very smooth and level. The sheaves were beaten, and then the straw was taken away, and the grain and chaff below it was winnowed. By this the chaff was blown away and only the grain was left.

When Boaz winnowed his barley Naomi told Ruth to go down to his threshing floor and see him for he had a feast for his friends.

So after the feast Ruth came near to him and said,

"Thou art our near kinsman," and Boaz said,

"May the Lord bless thee my daughter," and with many kind words he gave her six measures of barley to take to Naomi.

Boaz remembered that it was the custom in Israel for the nearest relative of a man who had died, to take care of the wife who was left, and so he went to the gate of Bethlehem where the rulers met to hold their court, and spoke to the elders and chief men about Ruth. He also wished them to be witnesses that he was going to take Ruth to be his wife. Then the rulers all said,

"We are witnesses," and they prayed that God would bless Ruth and make Boaz still richer and greater.

So Ruth became the honored and beloved wife of Boaz, and they had a son named Obed.

Obed grew up and had a son named Jesse; and Jesse was the father of David, King of Israel, who was first a shepherd lad of Bethlehem.

RUTH AND NAOMI.

More than a thousand years after Ruth lived there was born in Bethlehem, of the family of Boaz and Ruth, a little Child, who came to be the Saviour of the world, and the shepherds in the fields, where, perhaps, Ruth gleaned, and David kept his sheep, heard the angels tell the good news and sing

"Peace on earth, good will to men."

CHAPTER XVIII.

SAMUEL—THE CHILD OF THE TEMPLE.

The Tabernacle that was built in the wilderness, and was brought into Canaan by the priests was set up at Shiloh in the very centre of the land of Canaan, and once every year the tribes came to it to worship and offer sacrifices. After it had come to Shiloh to stay it was called the temple.

When Eli was high priest a man named Elkanah came up from Ramah to worship, and Hannah his wife went with him. She was a good woman, and very sorrowful, because she saw other wives with sons and daughters around them, and she had none. Her husband was loving and kind and said: "Am I not better to thee than ten sons?" but she prayed to God for a son. While she was at Shiloh she prayed in the temple, and Eli saw her lips move, though he heard no voice. At first he spoke harshly to her, thinking she had been drinking wine, but she told him that she had not taken wine, but was praying.

"I am a woman of sorrowful spirit," she said, "and have poured out my soul before the Lord." Then Eli blessed her and said:

"Go in peace, and the God of Israel grant thee the prayer that thou hast asked of him." Then Hannah was no longer sad.

Her prayer was answered, and the Lord sent her a little son, and when he was old enough, she took him to the temple, for she had promised the Lord that the child should be His. So Elkanah came bringing sacrifices, and the young child was with them. Hannah told Eli that she was the woman whom he saw praying in the temple.

"For the child I prayed," she said, "and the Lord has answered my prayer. Therefore I have lent him to the Lord; as long as he lives he shall

be lent to the Lord." Eli was very glad and gave thanks to the Lord, and took the little boy to help him in the service of the temple. Every year his father and mother came to bring offerings to the Lord, and his mother always brought him a little coat which she had made.

Over it was a linen garment called an ephod, such as the priests wore. Eli was an old man, and his sons, though they were priests, were not good men, and he believed the Lord had sent him one who would be good, so he loved little Samuel as if he were his own.

One night when Eli was laid down to sleep, and Samuel also, while the light was still burning in the golden candlestick before the Ark, Samuel heard a voice calling him, and he answered, "Here am I," and ran to see what Eli wanted. But Eli said that he had not called, and Samuel lay down again. When the voice called again, Samuel went again to Eli's bed, but Eli told him to lie down again, for he had not called him. When the voice called the third time, Samuel said: "Here am I, for thou *didst* call me."

Then Eli told the boy to lie down once more, but if he heard the voice again to say,

"Speak Lord, for thy servant heareth."

And when the voice called again, "Samuel, Samuel," the boy answered, "Speak Lord, for thy servant heareth."

Then the Lord told Samuel that the sons of Eli had become very wicked, and their father had not kept them from the evil, and therefore He could not accept their offerings.

When Eli asked Samuel what the Lord had said to him, the boy told him all and hid nothing from him, and Eli bowed his spirit before the Lord, and said:

"It is the Lord, let Him do what seemeth Him good."

After this all the people of Israel knew that the Lord had called Samuel to be a prophet. And as he grew up the Lord was with him, and he was a judge over his people all his life.

As for Eli and his sons, the word of the Lord soon came true. When the Philistines came against the Israelites in battle, the Elders of Israel said "Let us bring the Ark of the Lord out of Shiloh to us, that it may save us out of the hand of our enemies." And so they took it from the holy place to the camp of Israel. Then the Philistines fell upon the camp and scattered the men of Israel. They also took the Ark of God, and the two sons of Eli were among the thousands slain.

Eli, who trembled for the Ark of God, sat outside the city gate, by the wayside watching. He was nearly a hundred years old, and his eyes were dim, but when a messenger came with the bad news, he fell backward in his seat and died. His heart was broken.

Where was Samuel? Perhaps he was praying in the temple for the return of the Ark of the Covenant.

Wherever the Ark went among the Philistines, there went also trouble and death. When they put it in the temple of their fish-god Dagon, the great idol fell down before it and was broken. And when it was taken to another city, the people were smitten with sickness, until at last the Philistines said:

"Send away the Ark of the God of Israel, and let it go to its own place."

After seven months they sent it with gifts of gold to the Israelites. They placed it on a new cart drawn by two cows, and the cows, guided by the Lord alone, took a straight way into the land of Israel. How glad the people were when they looked up from their reaping in the fields, and saw the Ark coming safely back to them. The Philistines watched it from afar to see if it would be guided of God to its own place or not and then they returned to their city.

Samuel gathered the people to the Lord after this, and though they had sinned greatly, and had gone after the gods of the heathen around them, they repented and returned to the faith of their fathers, and were faithful all the days of Samuel. He went from year to year on a journey to three cities of Israel, and judged the people in those places, but his home was in Ramah, the city where he was born, and where Hannah had brought him up for the Lord.

CHAPTER XIX.

THE MAKING OF A KING.

When Samuel was old he made his sons judges in his place, but they were not holy men like their father.

They loved money, and would judge unjustly, if money were given to them as a bribe. So the people came to Samuel at Ramah and said,

"Give us a king to judge us."

And Samuel prayed to the Lord, and the Lord told him to do as the people had asked him to do, for they had not rejected him as judge, but the Lord as their King, and now they must learn what kind of a king would reign over them. So Samuel told them what they must be ready to do for their King, for a king was often a hard master, and ruled his people cruelly, taking the best of their fields, and their harvests, and their flocks for themselves, and the finest of their sons and daughters to be his servants; but they said,

"We will have a king over us, that we may be like other nations, and that our king may judge us, and go out before us and fight our battles."

When Samuel told these things to the Lord he said, "Make them a king," and Samuel sent the people to their own cities.

Samuel did not choose a king for the people himself, but he waited for the Lord to send him the man He had chosen, and the Lord said to him as he went to a city called Zeph, to hold a sacrifice,

"To-morrow about this time I will send thee a man from the land of Benjamin, and thou shalt anoint him to be captain over my people Israel."

On the next day as Samuel came out to go up to the hill of sacrifice he met a tall, noble looking young man, who, with his servant, was looking for the lost asses of his father, Kish, the Benjaminite. He had come far, and had heard that Samuel, the seer was in that place, and he hoped he would tell him where to go for the asses that were lost.

Samuel knew from the Lord that this was the man God had chosen, so he told him to go up with him to the sacrifice, and the next day he would let him go.

He told him that he need not be troubled about the asses, for they were found, but the desire of Israel was set upon him. Saul, for that was his name, did not understand him until he was invited to feast with thirty of the chief men, and Samuel had talked with him upon the house-top. Early the next morning they both rose and went out of the city, and while Saul sent his servant on before, Samuel anointed Saul with oil, and kissed him saying, that the Lord had anointed him to be Captain over his inheritance.

As a sign that the Lord had done it, he told Saul three things that would happen to him on the way home, and charged him to go to Gilgal, where he would meet him and sacrifice to the Lord for seven days. As Saul turned to leave the prophet, God gave him another heart, and all the signs came to pass that day.

At Mizpah Samuel called all the tribes together, that the man who was to be their king, might be chosen in their sight, and when Saul, the son of Kish, the Benjaminite was chosen he could not be found; he had hidden from the people; but when they brought him out before them, he was taller than

THE SHEPHERD BOY OF BETHLEHEM.

any of the people from his shoulders up, and looked a king indeed. For the first time in all their history they cried,

"God save the King!"

Then Saul went home, and there went with him a body of men whose hearts God had touched, while Samuel wrote in a book the order of the kingdom and laid it up before the Lord.

CHAPTER XX.

THE SHEPHERD BOY OF BETHLEHEM.

After Saul had been king of Israel for a few years, Samuel was deeply troubled about him, for he had hoped that he would be as truly a king as he looked, but he had a strange and wilful spirit that led him to turn away from the counsel of the Lord and follow his own way.

Samuel had been grieved again and again by Saul's rashness, until at last he said to him when he had taken the spoil of the enemy to sacrifice to the Lord,

"To obey is better than sacrifice; because thou hast rejected the word of the Lord, He hath also rejected thee from being king," and he went to his house and mourned over Saul, for he had loved him.

At last the Lord told Samuel to cease from mourning for Saul, for He had rejected him, but to fill his horn with oil, and go to Bethlehem where Jesse lived, for He had chosen one of the sons of Jesse to be king in place of Saul.

Samuel went to Bethlehem leading a heifer, as the Lord had told him to do, that he might hold a sacrifice. He told the elders of the city to make ready for the sacrifice, and when he had found the house of Jesse, he called him and his sons. Jesse was the grandson of Ruth and Boaz, and owned the fields, no doubt, where Ruth gleaned. When Samuel saw Eliab, the son of Jesse, he said:

"Surely the Lord's anointed is before Him," but the Lord said:

"Look not on his countenance or on the height of his stature, because I have refused him, for the Lord seeth not as man seeth, for man looketh on the outward appearance, but the Lord looketh on the heart."

Then Jesse called Abinidab, but Samuel said:

"The Lord hath not chosen this." Then he made Shammah to pass before him, but Samuel said:

"Neither hath the Lord chosen this."

Jesse made seven of his sons to pass before Samuel, but Samuel said: "The Lord hath not chosen these."

"Are here all thy children?" said Samuel.

"There remaineth yet the youngest, and he keepeth the sheep," Jesse replied. Then Samuel said:

"Send and fetch him, for we will not sit down till he come hither."

So Jesse sent out into the sheepfolds on the hillsides outside the city to bring the lad David in. What did the boy think when he found his father and his brothers waiting, with the old prophet in the midst? What did it mean that the eye of the seer was set upon him, as were the eyes of all in the house?

Samuel saw a noble youth, "ruddy, and of a beautiful countenance, and goodly to look to." He had been told that he must not look on the outward appearance "for the Lord seeth not as man seeth," and so he waited a little until the Lord said:

"Arise, anoint him, for this is he." Then he took the horn of oil, and anointed him in the midst of his brethren, and the spirit of the Lord came upon David from that day forward, and Samuel went back to his house in Ramah.

It may be that his father and his brothers did not understand that the boy had been called to be king over Israel, but a new spirit of wisdom, and love, and strength came upon David, and though he went back to his father's flocks with no thought of being greater than his brothers, he went with a new song in his heart which he sang to the little harp he had made while watching the sheep. Long after when he was King of Israel, he made in memory of these days the beautiful Psalm to be sung in the temple beginning,

"The Lord is my Shepherd, I shall not want."

CHAPTER XXI.

THE POWER OF A PEBBLE.

Saul the sullen was still king over Israel, although he had departed from the Lord, and in His sight he was no longer a king. He was very gloomy and dark in his mind, for he had driven the Lord's spirit away, and his light was gone.

His servants tried to amuse him, and told him of David, the son of Jesse, who was a skillful player on the harp, and a brave and handsome youth. So Saul sent for David, and David, bringing presents from his father, came to the king's house.

Saul was greatly pleased with David, and asked Jesse to let his son stay with him, for when the evil spirit was upon him, if David played upon his harp the darkness left him. But this did not last, and after a while David went back to his flocks, and Saul forgot him.

Then the Philistines rose against Israel again. Their camp was on a mountain side, and Saul gathered his warriors on the side of another mountain and there was a valley between them.

Out of the Philistine camp a giant came one day, Goliath of Gath. He talked loud and often in order to terrify the Israelites, asking them to send out a man to fight with him, but he was not truly brave, for he had carefully covered his great body with armor of brass, so that no spear or sword could touch him. He defied Israel every morning and evening for forty days, and no one was found who would dare to go out alone to fight him. David's elder brothers were in camp, and Jesse, their father, called David from the flocks to take food to them. He found the army of Israel ready to go into battle, but Goliath came out as he had done each day and defied the Israelites, who ran in terror at the sight of him. The spirit of David was moved at this, and he said:

"Who is this Philistine that he should defy the armies of the living God?" "The man who killeth him," said one, "the King will enrich him, and, will give him his daughter and make his father's house free in Israel."

Then Eliab, David's eldest brother, spoke sternly to David asking him why he had left his sheep to come down and see the battle, and called him naughty and proud, but David still talked with the men, for the spirit of the

Lord was strong within him. When Saul heard of him and sent for him, David said:

"Let no man's heart fail because of him; thy servant will go and fight with the Philistine."

Saul frowned at David and said:

"Thou art not able to go against this Philistine; thou art but a youth, and he is a man of war."

Then David told the king how he had killed both a lion and a bear that had come down upon his father's flocks, and that he could also conquer the Philistine.

"The Lord that delivered me out of the paw of the lion, and the paw of the bear," said David, "He will deliver me out of the hand of this Philistine." And Saul said: "Go! and the Lord be with thee." Then Saul armed David with his own armor, but David said:

"I can not go with these, for I have not proved them," and he put them off.

And this was the way David armed himself to meet the giant.

He took his staff in hand, and chose five smooth stones from the brook and put them in his shepherd's bag, and with his sling in his hand, he drew near to the giant. Goliath came on also, his armor-bearer carrying the shield before him, but when he saw the youth David, he despised him, for he was without armor, or sword or spear, only his staff.

"Am I a dog, that thou comest to me with a staff," said Goliath, and then he told him that he would soon give his flesh to the birds and the beasts.

"Thou comest to me with a sword, and a spear, and a shield," said David, "but I come to thee in the name of the Lord of Hosts, the God of the armies of Israel whom thou hast despised."

Then the Philistine came down upon little David to destroy him, and David ran, not away from him, as the men of Israel had done, but straight toward him, taking a pebble from his shepherd's bag as he ran. Quickly putting it in the sling, he whirled it in the air once, twice, and then it went swift and straight to the mark. It sunk into the forehead of the giant, and he fell dead upon his face. Then David ran and stood upon the dead Philistine and cut off his head with the giant's great sword, and when the Philistines saw that their champion was really dead, they fled, pursued by the shouting hosts of Israel.

Saul had forgotten the youth who played upon the harp before him, for when he sent for him after the battle he said,

"Whose son art thou, thou young man?" and David answered,

"I am the son of thy servant Jesse, the Bethlehemite."

And Saul took him to live with him from that day.

CHAPTER XXII.

FAITHFUL UNTO DEATH.

Saul had a son named Jonathan, and he loved David as his own soul. He took off his princely robes, even to his sword, and his bow, and his girdle, and made David wear them; and David acted wisely in all that the king gave him to do. There was great joy and much feasting over the Death of Goliath and the flight of the Philistines, and wherever Saul went, the women came out of the cities to meet him, singing and dancing, and the song with which they answered one another was,

"Saul hath slain his thousands,
And David his tens of thousands."

Saul did not like this, and an evil spirit of jealousy came upon him, and he thought "What can he have more but the kingdom."

The next day the evil spirit came upon Saul in the house, and David played on his harp to quiet him, but Saul hurled a spear at David, hoping to fasten him to the wall with it. This he did twice, but the Lord guided the spear away from David, just as he guided the pebble to Goliath, and he was unhurt. Saul was afraid of David. He was afraid that God was preparing him to be king over Israel, so he sent him into battle, hoping he would be killed, but the life of David was in the Lord's hand, and no enemy could destroy it.

After a great battle, in which David had been victorious, the evil spirit came again upon Saul, as he sat in his house with his spear in his hand, while David played on the harp. Again he tried to kill David, but the spear struck the wall and David slipped away.

THE POWER OF A PEBBLE.

It was clear that David could not live near the king, and so he talked with Jonathan, his friend, who said,

"God forbid, thou shalt not die," but David said,

"Truly there is but a step between me and death."

Then they made a promise to each other before the Lord that should last while they lived. They promised to show "the kindness of the Lord" to each other while life should last.

Jonathan told David that he might go away for three days, and they went out into a field together. They feared the anger of Saul when he found that David was absent from the feast of the new moon. So Jonathan told David to return after three days and hide behind a great rock in the field. Then Jonathan said he would come out and shoot three arrows from his bow, as if he were shooting at a mark, and he would send his arrow-bearer to pick them up. If he should call to the lad, "The arrows are on this side of thee," David would know that Saul was not angry, and would not hurt him, but if he cried, "The arrows are beyond thee," David would know he was in danger and must go away.

On the second day of the feast, Saul asked why David was not there, and Jonathan told him he had asked permission to go away for three days. Then Saul was very angry. He blamed his son for loving David, for, as Saul's son, Jonathan should be king after his death, but he never would be if David lived, and he commanded Jonathan to bring him that he might put him to death. When Jonathan asked what evil David had done that he should be put to death, Saul cast his spear at his own son. Then Jonathan knew there was no hope for David, and left the table in sorrow.

The next day he went out to the rock in the field with his armor-bearer and sent him on before. When he shot an arrow, he cried:

"The arrow is beyond thee; make haste! stay not!"

And David, in his hiding place heard it, and knew that he must flee for his life.

Then Jonathan gave his bow and arrows to the lad to take to the town, and David came out from his hiding place, and they kissed each other and wept together. But at last Jonathan said:

"Go in peace: as we have sworn both of us in the name of the Lord, saying, The Lord be between me and thee, and between my children and thy children forever."

And David went away to hide from Saul, and Jonathan went back to the king's house.

For seven years Saul hunted for David to take his life, and David, often hiding in caves in the wilderness, could not see his friend Jonathan, but they were faithful in their friendship, and when at last Saul was slain in battle, and Jonathan also, David came to mourn over his friend, saying:

"I am distressed for thee, my brother Jonathan: very pleasant hast thou been unto me; thy love for me was wonderful, passing the love of women."

CHAPTER XXII.

DAVID THE OUTCAST.

For seven years King Saul hunted David from one end of the land of Israel to the other. The evil spirit of jealousy and hate had full possession of him, and David, with a few faithful men, was driven from one stronghold to another, until he cried, "They gather themselves together; they hide themselves; they mark my steps when they wait for my soul. What time I am afraid I will trust in thee."

He had escaped again and again from the hand of Saul, and now he was down in the desert country by the Dead Sea, hiding among the cliffs and caves of Engedi. Saul heard of it and took three thousand men to hunt for him among the rocks of the wild goats. He was very tired after climbing the rocks, and seeing a cave, he went in to lie down for a little sleep. He did not know that David and his men were in the cave hiding in the dark sides of it. Then his men whispered to David:

"Behold the day of which the Lord said unto thee: 'I will deliver thine enemy into thine hand that thou mayest do to him as it shall seem good to thee.'" Then David arose and crept near to Saul, and—did he kill the man who had so often tried to kill him?

No, he bent down and cut off a part of Saul's robe. Even this seemed wrong to David.

"The Lord forbid that I should do this thing unto my master," he said "to stretch forth my hand against him, seeing he is the annointed of the Lord," and in this way he kept his servants from harming Saul, and after Saul awoke he went out of the cave.

David also went out of the cave and cried,

"My Lord the King!"

THE GARMENT OF SAUL.

And when Saul turned David bowed down to him and asked him why he listened to men who said that he wished to harm the king, and then he told him how the Lord had given him into his hand in the cave, but he would not touch the Lord's annointed to harm him.

"See, my father," he cried "see the skirt of thy robe in my hand. I have not sinned against thee, yet thou huntest my soul to take it."

Much more he said, and asked the Lord to judge between them, and Saul's hard heart was moved so that he wept aloud.

"Is this thy voice, my son David," he said, "Thou art more righteous than I, for thou hast rewarded me good, whereas I have rewarded thee evil," and he made a covenant with David. For though he made no promise to spare David's life, he made David promise to spare the life of his children when he should be made king.

But a year was hardly past before the evil spirit was again upon Saul, and he went out with three thousand men to hunt for David. Saul's camp was on a hill, and David saw where it was. At night he took Abishai, one of his warriors, and went down from the cliffs to Saul's camp, where Saul lay sleeping in a trench, and the spear stuck in the ground by his pillow, while all his men lay around him. Abishai wished to strike him through with the spear, but David said,

"Destroy him not, for who can stretch forth his hand against the Lord's anointed and be guiltless? The Lord shall smite him, or his day shall come to die, or he shall fall in battle and perish; but take thou now the spear that is at his pillow, and the cruse of water, and let us go."

And they took them and went away. A deep sleep had fallen upon the camp of Saul from the Lord, so that no one saw them.

Then David went up to his stronghold, and from the top of the cliff he cried to Abner, the captain of Saul's men, and asked why he had not defended his Master, and where was the king's spear, and his cruse of water?

Then Saul cried as before,

"Is this thy voice, my son David?"

"It is my voice, my lord, O King," said David, and again he plead his cause with his old enemy, but who could trust to the repentance of Saul? He cried,

"I have sinned; return, my son David, for I will no more do thee harm, because my soul was precious in thine eyes this day. I have played the fool, and erred exceedingly."

But David trusted him no more, and went and made friends with a Philistine prince that he might live within their borders.

Samuel the prophet was dead, and there was no one to give counsel to the darkened soul of the King when trouble fell upon him. The Philistines had come with a great army, but Saul was afraid, for the Lord's spirit was not with him. He tried to seek the Lord through the priests, and through dreams, but the Lord answered him not. Then he went to a witch by night, and asked her to bring up the spirit of Samuel. The witch could not bring up Samuel, but the Lord sent him to speak to Saul, and the woman cried out with terror when she saw the prophet of the Lord, and knew also that it was the King who had called for him.

"I am sore distressed," said Saul, "and God is departed from me. What shall I do?"

Then Samuel told him plainly that the kingdom was taken from him and given to David, and that on the next day he and his sons should fall in battle, and the Israelites into the hands of the Philistines.

Saul, forsaken and despairing, fell to the earth fainting, but was revived by the woman, who gave him food so that he went away through the dark to the camp of Israel.

In the battle of the next day the Philistines conquered. The three sons of Saul were slain, and Saul himself, when chased by the Philistines, fell upon his own sword and died.

When a messenger brought news of the battle to David he rent his clothes for grief, and in the chant of lamentation that he made, he mourned for his faithful friend Jonathan, and had no word of blame for his enemy Saul, neither did he triumph over him.

CHAPTER XXIII.

EVERY INCH A KING.

After Saul's death David came back to live with his own people, for he was of the tribe of Judah. He went to Hebron, the old home of Abraham, Isaac, and Jacob, for the Lord had told him to go there, and the men of his tribe came to Hebron and anointed him king. The other tribes did not come, for Saul's son and the captain of his host, Abner, were still holding the kingdom. But when both were killed by an enemy, then all the other tribes came to Hebron and made a league with him, so seven years after Saul's death David became king over all Israel. He was then thirty years old and his reign lasted forty years.

Then David began to establish the kingdom. There was a rocky height not far from Hebron with a valley all around it that was still held by the Jebusites, one of the tribes of Canaan that the Lord said must not be left in the land. The city was Jerusalem, and the stronghold was Zion, and close by Zion was the mount to which Abraham had once gone to offer up Isaac. David wanted this stronghold for the chief city of the kingdom, and so he took it, and it became the city of David. He built a beautiful house for himself there, and King Hiram of Tyre sent skilled workmen, and cedar trees, and they built a house of cedar for him. But stronger than the wish to have a house for himself was the longing to see the Ark of God set within the curtains of the Tabernacle in the city of David. It had been in the house of Abinadab in Kirjath-Jearim for seventy years, ever since it was sent home by the Philistines who captured it. Because the people had grown cold toward God, they did not wish to hear the reading of the law, or be led by his counsel. Now David called together the flower of all Israel, thirty thousand men, and they went to bring the Ark to the city of David. While on the way a man who had laid his hand upon the Ark when it was unsteady was smitten and died, for no one but the priests and Levites could touch the Ark of God. David feared to bring it further, and so he placed it in the house of Obed-edom which was near by. It was there three months, and great blessing came to the house because of it. When David heard this he went joyfully down to bring the Ark to his city, and it was with sacrifices, and shouting, and the sound of trumpet that it was brought and set in the Tabernacle that had been made ready for it. And so the worship of the Lord was established in Jerusalem, which was to be the great altar for the sacrificial worship until the sacrifice should be taken away, and the kingdom of Christ established on the earth.

But David was not satisfied.

"See," he said to Nathan the prophet, "I dwell in a house of cedar, but the Ark of God dwelleth within curtains."

That night the Lord spoke to Nathan and told him what to say to the king. He promised to establish the royal house of David, and give final peace to the people, and also to build a house for the worship of the Lord, but he said that David's son, who should be king after him, should build a house to his name, and of him the Lord said, "I will be his Father, and he shall be my son."

Then King David went in to the Tabernacle and thanked the Lord for His promise to him and to his son, and asked His blessing upon them. Though he reigned forty years, he never forgot that his work was not to build the temple of the Lord, but to prepare for it. So he subdued enemies, built cities, made leagues with friendly nations, gathered much wealth of wood, and stone, and gold, and silver and precious stones for the house of the Lord, and trained choirs of singers for the service. He also kept his heart open toward the Lord, so that he was able to write some wonderful poems that were set to music and sung by the temple choirs. We call them the Psalms of David.

Though David had grown rich and great, he did not forget his promise to Jonathan. He called Ziba, who had been Saul's servant and said to him,

"Is there not yet any of the house of Saul that I may show the kindness of God to him?"

Then Ziba told him of a man who was lame in both his feet, who was the son of Jonathan. David sent for him, and gave him all the land of Saul, and a place was made for him at the king's table among his own sons, and it was his while he lived.

CHAPTER XXIV.

DAVID'S SIN.

The army of Israel was at war with the Ammonites, and Joab was the chief captain. David did not go out with the army, but stayed in his house in Jerusalem. One evening he was walking on the flat roof of his house, as the people of that country always do, and he saw a little way off a very beautiful woman. He sent a servant to ask who she was, and found she was the wife of Uriah who was in the army with Joab, fighting the Ammonites. Then a great temptation was set before David, and instead of going to the Lord to be saved from it, he sent to Joab, asking him to send him Uriah, the Hittite. So Uriah came, and David talked kindly with him, and found him a good and faithful man. When he went back to Joab he took a letter from David, who asked that he be set in the front of the battle. So Joab placed him there, and when the two armies met Uriah was killed, and Joab sent a messenger to tell David. After her mourning was ended, Bathsheba, the wife of Uriah, became the wife of David, but the Lord was displeased with David. He also knew David's heart and how to deal with him, so he sent Nathan the prophet to him.

"There were two men in one city," said Nathan, "one of them rich and the other poor. The rich man had many flocks and herds, but the poor man had nothing, save one little ewe lamb, which he had bought and nourished up; and it grew together with him and with his children: it did eat of his own meat and drink of his own cup, and lay in his bosom and was unto him as a daughter. And there came a traveller unto the rich man, and he spared to take of his own flock to dress for the wayfaring man that was come to him, but took the poor man's lamb and dressed it for the man that was come to him."

David was very angry at the man who could do such a cruel thing, and he said to Nathan,

"The man that hath done this thing shall surely die; and he shall restore the lamb fourfold, because he did this thing, and because he had no pity."

Then Nathan said to David, "Thou art the man," and he told him how greatly the Lord had blessed him in making him King over Israel, and in delivering him from the hand of Saul, and how he had slain a faithful servant and taken his wife for himself; therefore evil would befall him.

David said, "I have sinned against the Lord," and the Lord saw that his repentance was real, and forgave the sin, but that David might never forget and sin again, the Lord took the little child that was born to him and to Bathsheba. While it was sick David fasted and lay all night upon the earth, and would not rise to taste food. This he did for seven days while the little child was sick, but when they told him that his child was dead he arose and bathed and dressed himself and went to the house of the Lord to worship, and returned to take his food. Then his servants wondered at it, and replied,

"While the child was yet alive I fasted and wept, for I said, who can tell whether God will be gracious unto me that the child may live. But now he is dead, wherefore should I fast? Can I bring him back again? I shall go to him, but he shall not return to me."

After this another child was born to Bathsheba, and they named him Solomon, which means "Peaceable."

And David wrote a prayer of repentance for his sin. It is the fifty-first Psalm, and has been the prayer of penitent souls for nearly three thousand years.

CHAPTER XXV.

DAVID'S SORROW.

David had a very beautiful son named Absalom. From the crown of his head to the soles of his feet there was no fault to be seen in him. His hair was thick and long, and his beauty was much talked of through all Israel. But the Lord who looks upon the heart saw that the heart of Absalom was wicked and false. He killed his brother Amnon, and then fled to another country and stayed three years. When he returned he tried to see his father, but David would not see him for two years. Then Absalom forced Joab to bring him to the king's house by setting Joab's barley field on fire. He was false as well as handsome, and won his father's heart by pretending to be humble.

After this Absalom began to live more like a king than a prince. He had fifty men to run before his chariot when he rode, and he stood in the city gates and talked with the men who came to see the king about their rights. He told them that if he were ruler over the land every man should have all that he wanted, and deceived many by a false show of friendship.

Then he asked the king if he could go to Hebron to pay a vow to the Lord by offering sacrifice there, and David told him to go in peace, and he went. But he had cruelly deceived his father. He had sent spies through all the land to persuade them to join him at Hebron and make him king. He also took two hundred men out of Jerusalem to help him, and one of them was David's counsellor. They had arranged to have all the people, as soon as they heard anywhere the sound of the trumpet, to cry,

"Absalom is king in Hebron."

Then it came to the ears of David that his people had been led away by deceit to follow Absalom, and David, who had been fearless before Goliath and before great armies of other nations, was afraid. His heart was broken at the treachery of his son, and he said to his servants,

"Arise, and let us flee; make haste and go, for fear Absalom may come and fight against the city with the sword."

His servants were ready to fight for him, but he fled in haste over the brook Kedron and went toward the wilderness, with all of the people of the city with him, until there was a great multitude, and in the midst the priests and the Levites bearing the Ark of God, but when David saw this he said,

SAUL ATTEMPTS THE LIFE OF DAVID.

"Carry back the Ark of God into the city. If I shall find favor in the eyes of the Lord He will bring me again. Let Him do to me as seemeth good to Him."

So the priests and the Levites returned to the city with the Ark of God.

It was a sad procession that went over the Mount of Olives led by David, weeping as he went, with his head covered and his feet bare. Some enemies of the house of Saul came out and troubled him by the way, but there was no anger in the heart of David toward any. He believed the hand of the Lord was upon him, and he said,

"It may be the Lord will look on mine affliction."

Absalom came to Jerusalem, and while he was asking his chief counsellor what to do, he was persuaded by a friend of David, who had stayed behind, to wait until he had gathered a larger army before he followed after David. This gave him time to send word to David to cross over Jordan before Absalom should overtake him. The chief counsellor, when he saw that his advice was not followed, went to his own house and hanged himself, for he knew that the Lord was bringing his counsel to naught.

After David had passed over into Gilead the people of that land brought food, and dishes, and beds to the sorrowful king and his tired people, and they were cared for in the city of Mahanaim. Then Joab, the captain, gathered the men together to go and meet Absalom and his army, and as they passed out of the city David stood in the gate and charged all the captains as they passed, saying

"Deal gently, for my sake, with the young man, even with Absalom."

So they went out to battle, and it was in a wood. God had given David's army the victory, and twenty thousand men of Absalom's army were slain. Absalom, who rode on a mule, was caught by his long thick hair in the branches of an oak tree, and the mule went away and left him hanging there.

A man ran and told Joab that he had seen Absalom hanging in an oak.

"Why didst thou not smite him there?" said Joab.

The man said he would not have done it for a thousand shekels of silver, because David had charged them all not to touch the young man Absalom.

But Joab turned away, and when he had found Absalom in the oak, he, with the ten young men who were with him, killed Absalom, and they buried him in the wood.

Then Joab sent two messengers to carry news of the victory to the king, who sat between the city gates, while a watchman stood over the gates on the

THE DEATH OF ABSALOM.

city wall. When the watchmen saw the two men running, one after the other, he cried out and told the king. The first man cried as he came, "All is well," but when the king said, "Is the young man Absalom safe?" he could not answer, and when the second messenger cried, "Tidings, my lord, the king," again David asked,

"Is the young man Absalom safe?"

The enemies of my lord the king and all that rise against thee to do thee hurt be as that young man," said the messenger.

Then the king went up to the room over the city gate and wept, and as he went he cried,

"O my son Absalom! my son, my son Absalom! would God I had died for thee, O Absalom, my son, my son!"

The people who had come back joyful because the enemy had been conquered were distressed by the grief of the king, so that Joab persuaded David to come down to the gate and meet the people.

After this those who were left of the followers of Absalom begged the king to come back to Jerusalem, and so he came, and thousands came to meet him. He had only forgiving words for those who had injured him, and for Barzillai and the men of Gilead who had fed them and shown them great kindness in the darkest hour of the king's life, and who came a little way on the journey with them, he had grateful words and blessings.

And so the king came to his own again. He was now getting to be an old man, and the love of his people made his last days blessed.

His warriors said, "Thou shalt go no more out with us to battle, that thou quench not the light of Israel."

Once he sinned against the Lord by numbering his people. He wanted to know how many men in his kingdom could bear arms in battle, and he forgot that victory over the enemy was not with the many or the few, but with the Lord, who is the strength of his people. When he saw that he had done wrong he confessed it and begged for forgiveness, but a pestilence spread over all the land, and came near to Jerusalem, and the angel was stayed by the Lord's hand just over the threshing floor of Araunah. This was the broad flat top of Mount Moriah where long before Abraham had built an altar on which to offer Isaac.

When David saw the angel he said,

"I have done wickedly, but these sheep, what have they done? Let Thine hand, I pray thee, be against me, and against my father's house."

Then the prophet Gad said, "Go up, rear an altar to the Lord in the

DAVID MOURNING FOR ABSALOM.

threshing-floor of Araunah," and David went as the Lord commanded.

When they reached the mount Araunah offered David the piece of ground with the oxen for a sacrifice, but he would not take them as a gift.

"But I will surely buy it of thee at a price," said David, "neither will I offer burnt offerings to the Lord my God of that which doth cost me nothing."

So he bought the piece of ground and paid for it six hundred shekels of gold. Twice had the Lord blessed this spot with a miracle of salvation, and twice an altar had been built there, and looking upon it, David said,

"This is the house of the Lord God, and this is the altar of burnt offering for Israel," and he prepared to build there the temple of Solomon,—the altar of the world.

CHAPTER XXVI.

THE BUILDING OF THE GOLDEN HOUSE.

The time was near when David must leave his people and go to his God, and his chief thought was about the house of the Lord that he had longed to build, that the Ark of God might be at rest, and that the people might have a place of worship for all time to come. He knew that his son Solomon was to build the temple, but he was still young, and David made ready as far as he could for the building of the house. There were men at work in the quarries, cutting great stones, and there were men in the forests of Lebanon cutting and hewing cedars, and others gathering iron and brass, and gold, and silver for the treasury of David. He also spent much time dividing the sons of Levi into companies, so that they could in turn serve with the priests in the temple, and ordering the times and manner of service, for he believed that this temple would be a house of prayer for all nations. David had been a man of war, for he had been called to destroy idol worship in the land of Canaan, and to make it the land of Israel, in which the one true God should be worshipped forever, but Solomon's reign was to be one of peace, and the Lord chose a man of peace to build his house.

David had another son, Adonijah, who tried to make himself king as Absalom did, but David heard of it, and had Solomon proclaimed king before his own death, lest trouble should arise after. When Adonijah heard the shouts of the people, and the sound of the trumpets he was afraid, and expected Solomon would kill him, but Solomon said if he would only show himself a good man no harm should come to him.

The last things that David did were to call his princes and chief men together and tell them that the Lord had promised many years before, that Solomon should build the house of the Lord during his reign; and also that his children's children should rule over Israel, and he begged them to keep the Lord's commandments, that they might keep the good land that had been given them.

He also charged Solomon before them all to serve God with all his heart, but if he failed to do so he would be cast off forever.

David gave Solomon all the plans and patterns for the house of the Lord, as the Lord had given them to him; also the gold and silver stored up for time of building. He also told the people, when he had called them together, what he had stored for the work of the temple, and asked them who were willing to give also. Then the people brought gifts, as they did when the Tabernacle was built, and gave them to the Lord. David led them in a great thanksgiving service, and they offered three thousand sacrifices.

Solomon was again anointed king in the presence of all Israel, and took the throne of David; and David died, honored and loved by his people, and he was buried in his own city.

When Solomon went to Gibeon to sacrifice the Lord came to him in a dream and said,

"Ask what I shall give thee."

Solomon was wiser than all the sons of David, and yet he did not feel himself to be so. He said,

"I am but a little child; I know not how to go out or come in, and thy servant is in the midst of a great people that cannot be numbered. Give therefore thy servant an understanding heart to judge thy people, that I may discern between good and bad, for who is able to judge this thy so great a people."

And the Lord said,

"Because thou hast asked this thing, and hast not asked for thyself long life, neither riches, nor the life of thine enemies, lo, I have given thee a wise and understanding heart, and I have also given thee that which thou hast not asked—both riches and honor; and if thou wilt walk in my ways as thy father David did, then I will lengthen thy days."

The Lord was true to his word. Solomon had wisdom beyond all the old and the learned men of his kingdom, and many came to him for counsel who were not of Israel, for he was famous among the nations. Some of these nations wished to be ruled by him, and brought him many precious things as gifts; they had been conquered by David, and now they wished to be ruled by Solomon. He had thousands of servants and he knew how to direct their work. Away up in the mountains of Lebanon they worked with the servants of Hiram, King of Tyre, getting the cedar timbers ready for the temple, while Hiram's artisans in gold, and silver, and brass, and fine linen came to Jerusalem to work on the temple, and Solomon sent Hiram wheat, and olive oil, and wine. So wise were the workers in stone and wood that when the temple was built there was no sound of a hammer or any tool heard on Mount Moriah. Each stone was ready to fit into its place, and each piece of wood to fit another.

The house was not like any that we have ever seen. It was not large, but it was very precious. The cedar boards that lined the walls were carved in flower patterns, and covered with gold. The floor also was covered with gold. He divided the temple in two parts, as the Tabernacle had been, with a rich curtain of blue and purple and crimson. The innermost room was called the most holy place, and was for the Ark, and its walls were beautiful with cherubim, and palm trees, and flowers, overlaid with gold, as was the floor also. Within this most holy place stood two cherubim fifteen feet high. They were of olive wood covered with gold, and they stood with wings spread forth so that they touched each other, and also touched the wall on either side, and their wings overshadowed the mercy seat where the Ark of the Lord was to rest. All the carvings upon wood were covered with gold, and precious stones were set among them for light and beauty.

Solomon's workmen made two great pillars of brass to stand before the house, and a great brass altar for the burnt offerings. They also made ten basins of brass that were set upon wheels, and one very great one called the "sea" which stood on twelve brass oxen.

They also made many things for the use of the temple—candlesticks, and spoons, and censers all of pure gold, and there was also a golden altar and a golden table.

Solomon was seven years building the house of the Lord, and when it was finished, and its outer courts made ready, he called all the elders and chief men of Israel together to carry the Ark of God to its place. So the Ark, borne by the priests, and holding the tables of the law, was carried into the most holy place, and set under the wings of the cherubim. After the priests came out a cloud filled the house of the Lord so that the priests could not go in. It was the glory of the presence of the Lord.

Then Solomon stood before all the people and gave thanks to God and asked him to take the temple for his own house to dwell in, and kneeling down, he prayed that wherever the children of Israel might be, at home, or captives in a strange land, that the Lord would hear them when they prayed toward his house, and that all prayer offered in it might be heard and answered.

Then fire from heaven fell upon the great altar, and the sacrifice was consumed, and all over the great pavement of the court the people bowed and worshipped the Lord, saying, "For He is good, and His mercy endureth forever."

There were offerings and feasting for fourteen days, and then the people went to their homes to think of the wonderful things they had seen. And there were sacrifices offered morning and evening each day, on the Sabbath, and at the three great feasts of the year—the feast of the passover, the feast of the harvest, and the feast of tabernacles.

Solomon also built a wonderful house for himself, and another called the "house of the forest of Lebanon," where he kept his armor. The roof was upheld by cedars of Lebanon, standing like mighty pillars beneath it. So famous did his work and his wisdom become that a queen from a distant land called Sheba came to visit him. She came with a caravan of servants and camels bringing costly presents of spices, and gold, and precious stones. She asked him many things that she had longed to know, and he answered all her questions, and told her strange and wonderful things, so that after she had seen all his palace, and his servants, and the service of his table, and the beautiful ascent by which he went up to the temple, she said that the half had never been told her in her own country. They exchanged costly presents, and she went back to her own land.

Solomon had many ships upon the sea that brought riches from every land. He learned much of the world in this way, and as he grew older and from his throne of gold and ivory judged his people, he dropped many wise sayings that were written in a book by the scribes and are now called the "Proverbs of Solomon."

But in Solomon's latter days his wives, who were daughters of heathen kings, turned his heart from the Lord. When his father sinned he repented at once, and his heart never turned to idols, but with all his wisdom, Solomon was weak of will, and built temples for his wives to worship idols in.

THE QUEEN OF SHEBA BEFORE SOLOMON.

The Lord had made a promise to David that his sons should inherit the throne, and He kept the promise, but he allowed the kingdom to be divided. The two tribes who lived near to Jerusalem—Judah and Benjamin—were left to Solomon's son Rehoboam, but the ten tribes chose a man named Jeroboam to be their king. The men of Rehoboam, led by their king, went out to fight with the ten tribes, but the Lord would not let them. He spoke to them through a prophet and they went home.

So now there were two kings in Israel, and Rehoboam's kingdom was called the kingdom of Judah, and that of Jeroboam was called the kingdom of Israel; but after the kingdom was divided no kings ever reigned who could be compared with David and Solomon.

CHAPTER XXVIII.

ELIJAH THE GREAT HEART OF ISRAEL.

During the reign of Jehoshaphat, fourth king of Judah, and Ahab, sixth king of Israel, after the division of the kingdom, there came out of Gilead Elijah, a prophet of the Lord. Two of the kings of Judah, and all of the kings of Israel had been wicked men, and the Lord sent Elijah to Ahab, king of Israel, to tell him that there should be no rain for years in the land of Israel, and then only as Elijah should ask for it. Ahab was more wicked than the kings that reigned before him, and had built a temple for the god Baal in Samaria.

Because he would seek to destroy Elijah, the Lord told His prophet to go to the brook Cherith that ran into the Jordan, and there He would take care of him. "Thou shalt drink of the brook, and I have commanded the ravens to feed thee there," said the Lord.

And so it was. Morning and evening the ravens came bringing bread and meat, and the brook brought him water out of the rock, but as there was no rain, the brook at last dried up, and there was a great famine.

Then Elijah was told to go to Zarephath, for a woman there had been told to feed him, and he went at once. As he came near the city gate he saw a woman gathering sticks, and he asked her to bring him a cup of water and a little bread. She told him that she had but a handful of meal in a barrel, and a little oil in a cruse, and she was going to bake it for herself and son, that they might eat it and die.

Then Elijah said, "Fear not ; go and do as thou hast said, but make me thereof a little cake first, and after that make for thee and thy son, for thus saith the Lord God of Israel, 'The barrel of meal shall not waste, neither shall the cruse of oil fail until the day that the Lord sendeth rain upon the earth.'"

She believed Elijah, and did as he commanded, and they ate for a whole year, and the meal and the oil lasted all that time.

After this the woman's son grew very sick, so very sick that he appeared to be dead, and the woman cried to the prophet in her distress,

"O thou man of God, art thou come unto me to call my sin to remembrance and to slay my son?"

Then he said, "Give me thy son," and he took him up to his own room and laid him upon his bed and prayed over him. Then he stretched himself upon the child three times and cried,

"O Lord my God, I pray Thee let this child's soul come unto him again!"

And God heard Elijah, and the soul of the child came to him again, and he revived.

Then he gave the boy to his happy and grateful mother, saying, "See, thy son liveth."

In the third year of the famine the Lord said to Elijah,

"Go, show thyself to Ahab, and I will send rain on the earth."

As Elijah went he met a good man named Obadiah, who was governor of the king's house. This man worshipped the Lord, and when Ahab's wicked wife, Jezebel, tried to kill all the Lord's prophets he hid a hundred of them in two caves and kept them alive with bread and water. He was seeking grass and water for the king's horses, and when he saw Elijah he fell on his face and said,

"Art thou my Lord Elijah?"

"I am," said Elijah, "go, tell thy lord, 'Behold, Elijah is here.'"

Obadiah was in distress at this command, for he knew that the king would kill Elijah if he found him, and he could not think that Elijah would be brave enough to meet the king, or he thought perhaps the spirit of the Lord would carry him away, and he alone would have to meet the anger of the king.

"As the Lord of hosts liveth," said Elijah, "I will surely show myself unto him to-day."

So Obadiah told Ahab, and Ahab went to meet Elijah, and said to him, "Art thou he that troubleth Israel?"

"I have not troubled Israel," he said, "but thou and thy father's house, in that ye have forsaken the commandments of the Lord, and thou hast followed Baalim."

Then he told Ahab to call all Israel to Mount Carmel which overlooks the sea, and to bring there also the four hundred and fifty prophets of Baal, and the four hundred prophets of the groves.

So the king called them together, and Elijah cried to the people, "How long halt ye between two opinions? If the Lord be God, follow Him; but if Baal, follow him."

And the people, afraid of the king and his wicked wife, answered not a word.

"I, even I only, remain a prophet of the Lord," said Elijah, "but Baal's prophets are four hundred and fifty men." And then he told the people how it could be proven which was true—the God of Israel, or Baal.

He told the prophets of Baal to make an altar and place wood and a sacrifice upon it, and he also would do the same, and they should call upon Baal, and he would call on the name of the Lord, and "the God that answereth by fire, let him be God."

This the priests of Baal were willing to do, and they cried around their altar from morning until night, "O Baal, hear us," but there was no voice, and no answer by fire.

Elijah watched and waited, sometimes telling them that perhaps their god was asleep, and could be waked; or that he had gone on a journey, or was talking with somebody, and then they became wild and leaped upon the altar and cut themselves with knives.

After many hours Elijah called the people to him, and he repaired a broken altar of the Lord that stood there with twelve stones for the twelve tribes of Israel, and made a trench all around it. Then he placed wood on the altar and told the people to pour four barrels of water over the sacrifice. This they did three times, and the water ran down and filled the trench around the altar, and the people saw that Elijah could not by any means make a fire there.

Then, as it was the hour of the evening sacrifice in the temple, Elijah knelt by his altar with his face toward Jerusalem, and prayed to his God that He would hear him, and show the people that they were called from the worship of idols to the service of the living God.

What a wonderful sight was that, when fire fell from heaven and burnt up the sacrifice, and the wood, and the altar, and even the water in the trench around the altar!

And the people all fell on their faces at the sight, and cried,

"The Lord He is the God! The Lord He is the God!" Then Elijah told them to take the prophets of Baal and destroy them, and they did so.

"There is a sound of abundance of rain!" said Elijah to the king, and then he went to the very top of Carmel, and threw himself upon the earth, hiding his face between his knees, while he sent his servant to look toward the sea, and watch for the coming of the rain.

This the servant did seven times, each time coming to his master and saying, "There is nothing," but the prophet told him to look seven times more, and when he came back the seventh time he said,

"Behold, there ariseth a little cloud out of the sea like a man's hand."

Then he sent his servant to Ahab, saying,

"Prepare thy chariot and get thee down, that the rain stop thee not."

The little cloud grew to be a great one, and filled all the sky until it was black with clouds and wind, and there was a great rain. And as Ahab rode in his chariot, Elijah, who was strong with the spirit of the Lord and glad for His great victory over sin, ran before the chariot to the gates of the city.

Jezebel the queen was furious when she heard that the priests had been destroyed. She sent word to Elijah that he would be treated the same way on the morrow, and so Elijah fled for his life, and leaving his servant in Beer-Sheba on the southern border of Israel, he went a day's journey into the wilderness. There he sat down under a juniper tree, and for the first time his heart grew weak within him.

"It is enough," he said, "Now, O Lord, take away my life, for am I not better than my fathers."

Perhaps he was discouraged because he was tired and hungry, for he fell asleep, and when he awoke it was because an angel touched him, saying, "Arise and eat," and he looked, and there was a cake just baked on the hot coals, and a bottle of water close beside him. So he ate and drank, but he was not yet rested, and he fell asleep again. The angel waked him the second time telling him to eat and drink, for the journey was too great for him. Then he ate and drank again, and went on the strength of that food forty days and forty nights, till he came to Horeb, the mount of God, where the Ten Commandments were given to Moses, and there he lodged in a cave.

ELIJAH AND THE ANGEL.

He was still gloomy and discouraged, and when the Lord said, "What doest thou here, Elijah?" he said,

"I have been very jealous for the Lord God of hosts, for the children of Israel have forsaken thy covenant, thrown down thine altars, and slain thy prophets with the sword, and I, even I only am left, and they seek my life to take it."

Then the Lord told him to go out and stand on the mount before the Lord, and he passed by. There was a great wind that split the mountains, and broke the great rocks, but the Lord was not in the wind, and after the wind an earthquake, but the Lord was not in the earthquake; and after the earthquake a fire, but the Lord was not in the fire; and after the fire a still, small voice.

When Elijah heard that, he wrapped his face in his mantle and stood at the door of the cave, and the Lord asked again, "What doest thou here, Elijah?" and Elijah answered him just as he did before.

Then the Lord told him to go back and anoint a new king over Syria, also a new king over Israel, and Elisha to be prophet in his place.

Elijah went, and he found Elisha ploughing with twelve yoke of oxen. He cast his mantle over Elisha, and Elisha followed him and became his servant.

When Elijah came back to his own country he found there had been war between Israel and Syria, and Ahab had grown hard of heart again. He and his wicked wife Jezebel had taken the vineyard of Naboth away from him because Ahab wanted it for a garden, and they had caused the death of Naboth, so when Elijah came he found Ahab in the vineyard, and said,

"Hast thou killed and also taken possession?" and he told him that he should die where Naboth died.

"Hast thou found me, O mine enemy!" cried the king.

"I have found thee," answered Elijah, and he spoke to him the word of the Lord, that he should be destroyed out of Israel with his whole family.

Then Ahab repented, and the Lord spared his life two years, but later his wife Jezebel came to a dreadful end, with the seventy sons of Ahab.

When the time came for the Lord to take his servant to himself, Elijah wished to be alone, but Elisha his servant would not leave him. He followed his master from one town to another until they came to the river Jordan. Then Elijah took off his mantle, and folding it, struck the waters and they were divided, so that they went over on dry ground. Then Elijah said,

ELIJAH AND THE CHARIOT OF FIRE.

"Ask what I shall do for thee," and Elisha prayed that a double portion of his Master's spirit might rest upon him.

"If thou see me when I am taken from thee it shall be so unto thee," he said, "but if not, it shall not be so."

And as they went there appeared a chariot of fire, and horses of fire, parting them from each other, and Elijah went up in a whirlwind to heaven. Now Elisha wished his master to know that he saw him, so he cried,

"My father, my father! the chariot of Israel and the horsemen thereof!" and he saw him no more.

Then he took Elijah's mantle that fell from him, and struck the waters of Jordan again, and they parted, and he went over, and he knew that the power of the old prophet's spirit had been given to him.

Fifty young men, sons of the prophets, saw him return, and they said,

"The spirit of Elijah doth rest on Elisha," and they bowed themselves to the ground before him.

CHAPTER XXIX.

THE LITTLE CHAMBER ON THE WALL.

Elisha did many wonderful things in the strength of the spirit that Elijah's God gave him. He changed the waters of Jericho, so that they were no longer poisonous, by casting salt in the spring.

He brought water for the thirsty armies of three kings who had gathered to battle, by telling them to dig ditches in a valley of Edom, and watch for the water to come, without wind or rain. When the morning dawned the valley was full of running water.

He helped a poor widow to pay a debt and take care of her two sons by telling her to borrow empty pots and pans of all her neighbors, and pour into them her one little pot of oil. The oil increased until all the pots and pans were full, and she had plenty to sell.

He saved the sons of the prophets from death by casting meal into the pot when a poisonous nut had been mingled with the food, and he fed a hundred people with the bread that was brought as a portion for himself.

But the most beautiful story in the life of Elisha is that of the Shun-amite mother and her son. The mother was a noble lady of Shun-em, who

THE FEEDING OF ELIJAH.

believed in God, and in the good man who passed her house so often, and she said to her husband,

"Let us make for him a little chamber on the wall." And so they did, and when Elisha came again he lodged there. He was grateful to these kind people, and asked the woman what he should do for her—if she would ask anything of the king, but she only said,

"I dwell among mine own people."

Then the prophet, knowing that she had no child, promised that she should have a son, and though it was hard to believe, the little son was sent to her, and she was very happy. But one day when he went out in the field where his father and his men were reaping, he cried out, "My head, my head!" and they carried him in to his mother. She held him in her arms until noon, and then he died and she laid him in the prophet's chamber. Perhaps the heat of the harvest time had been too great for one so young. Did the mother cry out and call her husband? No, she called for a servant and a donkey, and rode as fast as she could to Mount Carmel where Elisha was. His servant saw her coming, and Elisha sent him to meet her and ask if it was well with her and her husband and her child, and she said,

"It is well," though her heart was breaking.

"Did I ask a son of my lord?" she said as she came to Elisha and fell at his feet. Then he knew that the child was ill or dead, and he would have sent his servant to lay his staff on the child, but the mother cried,

"As the Lord liveth, and as thy soul liveth, I will not leave thee," and he arose and followed her.

When he came to the Shun-amite's house he went into his little room where the dead child lay upon his bed, and, shutting the door, prayed to the Lord. Then he stretched himself upon the child, and breathed upon him until life began to creep back into the little cold body, and when he had done this twice the child opened his eyes. Then Elisha called the mother, and when she had fallen at his feet in grateful joy, she took up her child and went out.

ELIJAH RAISES THE WIDOW'S SON.

CHAPTER XXX.

A LITTLE MAID OF ISRAEL.

There was war almost all the time between Israel and Syria. A band of Syrians from Damascus would often come into a village of Israel and take the people away for slaves. One little girl who was carried off by the Syrians became a slave in the house of a Syrian general called Naaman, and was a maid to Naaman's wife.

Naaman was a great man, and beloved by all, but he had a disease that could never be cured. It was leprosy. He could go about, but he could not touch others without giving them the disease which turns the skin white and dead, and finally eats the flesh away.

The little maid said to her mistress one day,

"Would God my lord were with the prophet that is in Samaria! for he would recover him of his leprosy."

When this was told to Naaman he talked with the king, who sent him to the king of Israel with a letter, but the king of Israel was angry.

"Am I God to kill and make alive, that this man doth send unto me to recover a man of his leprosy?" he cried, but when Elisha heard of it he said,

"Let him come now to me, and he shall know that there is a prophet in Israel."

So Naaman came with his horses and chariot to Elisha's house, but the prophet did not even come to the door, but sent his servant with this message,

"Go wash in Jordan seven times, and thy flesh shall come again to thee, and thou shalt be clean."

But Naaman went away in a rage. He expected Elisha to come out, and that there would be a fine scene while he called on the name of God, waved his hand over the leprous spots, and made a cure.

"Are not Abana and Pharpar, rivers of Damascus, better than all the waters of Israel? May I not wash in them and be clean?" he said.

Then some of his servants came near to him and said,

"My father, if the prophet had bid thee do some great thing, wouldst thou not have done it? How much rather, then, when he saith to thee, 'Wash and be clean.'"

Then he went down and dipped himself seven times in Jordan, and his flesh became like the flesh of a little child, and he was clean.

After this he, with all that were with him, went humbly back to Elisha and said,

"Now I know that there is no God in all the earth but in Israel." And he urged the prophet to take gifts from him, but he would not.

But Naaman begged of Elisha two mule-loads of earth to take to his own country. He wanted to build an altar upon it to worship the God of Israel, and he thought it must stand on the soil of Israel.

Did Naaman ever send the little maid of Israel to her home? We do not know, but surely he was kind to her in some way.

CHAPTER XXXI.

THE TWO BOY KINGS.

There were many kings over Israel from the days of Solomon until the time when they were carried away captives to Babylon. The kingdom was divided soon after Solomon's death, and a king reigned in Jerusalem over the kingdom of Judah, and another in Samaria over the kingdom of Israel. There were a few kings who tried to follow that which was right, but the most of them were men who were given to idolatry, and who did not help the people to remember the true God. The Lord sent them prophets to remind them of Him, but they were often driven away or ill treated. There were a few good kings of Judah, such as Asa and Jehoshaphat, and Hezekiah, and among them were two who became kings when they were very young.

When Ahaziah, King of Judah, was killed, his mother, who was a wicked woman, killed all his sons, that she herself might be queen. All but a baby boy who was hidden with his nurse in the temple, and tenderly cared for by the good high priest and his wife for six years. Then when he was seven years old the priests and the Levites brought out little Joash and anointed him king. They formed a guard all about him, and when the high priest had crowned him there was a great cry around the temple of "God save the King."

The old queen heard this and came to see what it meant. When she saw the little Joash standing by a pillar with a crown on his head she cried out that the people were plotting against her.

The people did by her as she had done by her grandsons—they took her life.

Then there was great rejoicing. The house of Baal was torn down, and the Lord's gold and silver brought back to the temple, and the good high priest began the worship of God in the temple after the manner of former days.

When Joash was old enough to understand he longed to make the temple beautiful again, for it was falling into decay, so he called for money throughout his kingdom. Everyone was asked to drop a silver piece in the chest that was set at the temple door, and more than enough was brought to re-build the temple, and while the high priest lived the king worshipped there with all the princes of Judah, but as soon as he died they went back to idol worship, and killed the new high priest in the court of the temple because he told them that the Lord would bring great trouble upon them. And so it came to pass in less than a year the Syrians came and killed the princes, and took away the gold and silver treasures of the temple. Joash himself became very sick, and his own servants took his life as he lay helpless.

It was quite different with little Josiah. He was only eight years old when he was crowned King of Judah, and he had no one so good as the high priest Jehoida, who was the teacher of Joash, to help him to do right. Even the holy writings that were given to Moses were lost, and the people did not ask to hear them read. But the Lord had not allowed His word to be destroyed, and when Josiah was having the temple repaired the high priest found the rolls of parchment on which the law was written, and sent it to the king by a servant of the king who was a writer. Josiah was full of interest in the ancient book, and wished to know what was in it, and his servant read it to him.

When he found that he and his people were not living as God had commanded in the law, he sent to inquire of the Lord what He would have them to do, and they went to Huldah, the prophetess. She told the king's messengers that a great calamity would fall upon the kingdom because they had turned away from the true God, but because the king's heart was tender and full of desire to follow the Lord, it should not come during his lifetime.

Then the king called all the chief men of Judah, and the people of the city, both great and small, with the priests and the Levites, to the Lord's house, and there he read in their hearing the word of the Lord. It was like a new book to the most of them, but they were ready to follow the king in making a solemn promise to the Lord to do His commandments, and bring back the true worship.

So they had a great feast of the passover, to which all the people came with offerings, and there was no passover in all the history of the kings of Judah and Israel that was like this one that was held in the eighteenth year of the reign of Josiah.

After he had prepared the temple for worship, and had destroyed the altars of the idols, he went out to meet the King of Egypt in battle and was killed, and there was a great mourning for him in all the land, for he had been a good king—kind to his people and faithful to his God. Jeremiah the prophet made a great lamentation for him, for he knew that one of Josiah's sons would be the last king of Judah, and that for their sins the people would be driven out of their own land to be captives in Babylon for seventy years.

CHAPTER XXXII.

THE FOUR CAPTIVE CHILDREN.

Nebuchadnezzar, King of Babylon, came with his armies and besieged Jerusalem, just as Jeremiah the prophet had foretold. He took the king and the princes of Judah captive, and carried away their precious things from the temple and the palaces into his own land, and put them in the temples of his gods. Before twenty years had passed the whole nation had been driven into captivity, and their holy house had been burned, and the ark of the covenant lost or destroyed. As the kingdom of Israel had also been scattered, the whole land lay desolate, and the walls of the cities were broken down.

When the King of Babylon first besieged Jerusalem he carried away the finest of the princely families to serve him. They were the flower of Jerusalem—young men of noble face and form; well taught in the learning of the Jews, and skilfull in the sciences of that time. They were also chosen for their natural ability to learn the language and the wisdom of the Chaldeans.

Among these were four boys named Daniel, Hananiah, Mishael and Azariah. The king gave these boys into the care of his chief officer, who set teachers over them and treated them very kindly, while the king sent them each day meat and wine from his own table. The Chaldeans offered these things to idols, and then ate of them themselves; they also used some meats for food that were unclean to an Israelite, so that the four children of Judah determined that they would not touch the king's meat and drink.

Daniel spoke to the chief officer about it, and though he had learned to love Daniel very much, he was afraid to have the boys refuse the king's food.

"I fear my lord the king," he said, "who hath appointed your meat and your drink, for why should he see your faces sadder than the children which are of your sort? Then shall ye make me endanger my head to the king."

But Daniel turned to Melzar, the steward, and begged him to prove them by giving them only vegetables to eat and water to drink for ten days, and "Then," said he "let our countenances be looked upon before thee, and the countenance of the children that eat of the portion of the king's meat: and as thou seest, deal with thy servants." And he proved them for ten days.

At the end of that time their faces were fatter and fairer than the faces of all the others who ate portions from the King's table, and they were allowed to eat the food they had chosen.

They also grew in wisdom and judgment. Daniel had the gift of understanding visions and dreams, and the gift came from God, and not from the study of magic. Among all the young men these four were most pleasing to the king, and they were called to the palace to stand before him.

Not long after this the king had a dream that seemed very wonderful to him, but he could not remember it. He called all his magicians, and astrologers, and wise men together, and told them that they must tell him what his dream was, and the meaning of it, or he would destroy them. There was no man wise enough to tell him, and he ordered that all the wise men of Babylon should be killed, Daniel and his friends among them.

Daniel asked the captain of the king's guard why the king was so hasty with his decree, and the captain told him.

Then Daniel went to the king and told him that if he would give him a little time he would tell him his dream and its meaning, and he went to his three friends and together they prayed the God of Heaven to show them the dream and its interpretation.

That night Daniel saw in a vision from God the same thing that the king had seen and had forgotten. It was a great image standing before the king, and shining like the sun. The head was of pure gold, the breast and arms of silver, and the rest of the body of brass; while the legs were of iron, and

the feet were part of iron and part of clay. As he looked a great stone cut from a mountain by unseen hands was hurled at the image, striking its feet and breaking them. Then the image fell and broke into pieces so fine that the winds blew them away, but the stone grew to be a great mountain that filled the earth.

Then Daniel gave thanks to God for showing him the dream, and went to the king.

He told the king that the God of Heaven alone had revealed the dream, for no man could know it, and he told him what the dream had been. He also told him that God had shown him the meaning: that the head of gold was the king himself, who reigned over the greatest kingdom on earth, but after him new kingdoms would rise, and the silver, the brass, the iron and the clay stood for these; but in the days of the kingdom of iron and clay the God of heaven would set up a kingdom which should never be destroyed, but it would destroy all the kingdoms that had gone before it. This kingdom—the great stone cut without hands from the mountain—meant the Kingdom of Christ.

The king was so astonished at Daniel's wisdom—for it was the dream he had forgotten brought back and interpreted—that he fell on his face before Daniel and reverenced the God of heaven. He made Daniel chief ruler in his realm and gave also great honors to his friends.

Nebuchadnezzar soon forgot God, for he set up a great golden image on the plain of Dura, and called a feast of dedication. He had all his princes and governors there, and his captains, and judges, and rulers. The musicians were there also, with many kinds of instruments, and a herald was there who cried in a loud voice the command of the king. It was a call to worship the golden image. At the first sound of the bands of music all were to fall down before the golden image, or failing to do so, be thrown into a fiery furnace.

Among the rulers were the three friends of Daniel, whose names had been changed by the king to Shadrach, Meshach, and Abednego. They did not fall before the golden image, and some jealous Chaldeans who saw them went and told the king. Then the king, who had a fiery temper, was angry, and sent for the three young men. He told them the bands should play again, and if they failed to worship the golden image they should be cast into the furnace, "and who is that God that shall deliver you out of my hands?" he asked.

DANIEL IN THE LIONS' DEN.

"We are not careful to answer thee in this matter," they said, "If it be so, our God whom we serve is able to deliver us from the burning fiery furnace, and he will deliver us out of thy hand, O king."

Then the king in a great rage called his mighty men to bind the young men, and after the furnace was heated seven times hotter than before, they were thrown in. So great was the heat that the men who threw them in were killed by it in the sight of the king. As he watched the great door of the furnace the king rose up and said,

"Did not we cast three men bound into the midst of the fire?"

"True, O king," said his lords and captains.

Then the king with his eyes fixed upon the glowing door of the furnace said,

"Lo I see four men loose, walking in the midst of the fire, and they have no hurt, and the form of the fourth is like the Son of God."

Then he went near the door of the furnace and cried,

"Shadrach, Meshach, and Abed-nego, ye servants of the most high God, come forth and come hither!"

Then they came out before the king and all the people, who saw that the fire had no power over their bodies, for no hair of their head was burned, and no smell of fire was upon their garments.

Then the king was very humble, and acknowledged the God of heaven, "because there is no other God" he said "that can deliver after this sort." And he promoted the young men to still higher places in his kingdom.

CHAPTER XXXIII.

THE MASTER OF THE MAGICIANS.

The Lord saw that the heart of Nebuchadnezzar was lifted up with pride because he was king of a great people, and had conquered many weaker nations. He was proud of his royal city, Babylon. The walls of Babylon were sixty miles in length, and in them stood one hundred brazen gates. There were wonderful palaces, and statues, and bridges, and gardens. The river Euphrates ran through the city, and near the king's palace was a hill covered with trees and flowering plants from many lands, called the Hanging Gardens.

Babylon was built on a plain, but the king had these gardens made for his wife, who had come from a country of hills.

The king was praised so much by the princes and rulers that he thought only of his own power and riches, and became proud and cruel. So the Lord sent him a dream. He saw a tree great and high, standing in the midst of a wide plain. It grew until it reached the heavens, and its branches spread to the ends of the earth. It was thick with green leaves, and heavy with fruit; the birds lived in it, and the beasts lay in its shadow, and all things living came to it for food. Then he saw an angel coming down from heaven crying.

"Hew down the tree, and cut off his branches; shake off his leaves, and scatter his fruit; let the beasts get away from under it, and the fowls from his branches; nevertheless, leave the stump of his roots in the earth, even with a band of iron and brass, in the tender grass of the field; and let it be wet with the dew of heaven, and let his portion be with the beasts of the grass of the earth; let his heart be changed from a man's, and let a beast's heart be given unto him, and let seven times pass over him."

This dream was given that the king might be taught that the Lord alone is King.

Daniel, named by the king Belteshazzar, was called to interpret the dream, and the Lord gave him power to do it.

"The tree that thou sawest," said Daniel, "it is thou, O king, that art grown and become strong; for thy greatness is grown and reacheth unto heaven, and thy dominion to the end of the earth."

Then Daniel told the king that he must be driven from men to dwell with the beasts of the field; to eat grass with the oxen, and be wet with the dews of heaven, until he had learned that the Most High rules in the kingdom of men, and gives to whosoever He will. But as the roots of the tree were left in the ground, so his kingdom should be preserved for him until he had learned that the heavens do rule.

At the end of a year the king's heart had not been made humble, for as he walked in his palace he said to himself:

"Is not this great Babylon that I have built for the house of the kingdom by the might of my power, and for the honor of my majesty?"

And while he yet spoke there fell a voice from heaven, saying:

"O, King Nebuchadnezzar, to thee it is spoken; the kingdom is departed from thee."

And within an hour the word of the Lord came true. For seven years he was without reason, and was an outcast from his kingdom. But at the end of that time his eyes were lifted to heaven and his reason returned, and his kingdom was restored to him, for he had learned that God alone is great, and "Those that walk in pride He is able to abase."

Belshazzar was the next king of Babylon. He made a great feast, and a thousand of his lords were bidden to sit around his tables in the great hall of the palace. While he drank the wine he thought of the holy vessels of gold and silver that his father had brought out of the Temple at Jerusalem, and he sent for them, and into these golden bowls that had been consecrated to the worship of God he poured wine and gave it to his princes and to his wives, while they praised the gods of gold, and silver, and wood, and stone.

While they were feasting, and laughing, and singing, there came a man's hand and wrote some strange words on the wall of the great hall where they sat. The king saw the hand as it wrote, and he was so much afraid that he trembled and grew very weak. He called for his wise men and they could not read the writing, but the queen remembered that in the time of Nebuchadnezzar there was a man whom he made master of the magicians because he had power to interpret dreams and make all doubtful things clear.

So Daniel was brought before the king, and the king told him that if he would read the writing on the wall he should be clothed royally and be made the third ruler in the kingdom.

"Let thy gifts be to thyself," said Daniel, "and give thy rewards to another, yet I will read the writing unto the king, and make known to him the interpretation."

Then Daniel reminded the king of that which fell upon his father Nebuchadnezzar, when he had grown proud and hard-hearted toward God and men, and, though he knew all this, he also had lifted himself up against the Lord of heaven, and had defiled the holy vessels of the Temple by drinking from them to gods which could neither see or hear, and because of this the message had been written on the wall. And this was the interpretation of the strange words,—

"God hath numbered thy kingdom and finished it. Thou art weighed in the balances, and art found wanting. Thy kingdom is divided, and given to the Medes and the Persians."

The king clothed Daniel in scarlet, and gave him a chain of gold, and proclaimed him third ruler in the kingdom, but the same night Belshazzar was slain, and Darius the Median took the kingdom.

The new king set one hundred and twenty princes over the kingdom, and over these he set three presidents, the first of which was Daniel. The king

THE HANDWRITING ON THE WALL.

loved Daniel for the wise and good spirit that was in him, and this stirred up jealousy in the hearts of the Babylonian princes, and they watched Daniel to see if they could find something against him to tell the king, but they could not, for he was faithful in all his work.

Then they agreed to plot against him, and they went to the king and persuaded him to make a decree that whoever should ask any petition of any god or man for thirty days, except of the king, he should be thrown into the den of lions, and they asked the king to sign the decree, so that it could not be changed, and he signed it.

When Daniel heard of the decree, and knew that the king had signed it, he went into his own house, and to his chamber. There the windows were always open toward Jerusalem, and he kneeled down as he had done every day since he was taken from his own land, and prayed to God with his face toward the Temple in Jerusalem. And the men who were plotting against him watched him.

Then they hurried to the king, saying,

"That Daniel, which is of the captivity of Judah, regardeth not thee, O, King, nor the decree that thou hast signed, but maketh his petition three times a day."

The king was greatly disturbed at this, and set his heart on the deliverance of Daniel, and labored till sunset to do it. But his princes said it could not be done, because, according to the law of the Medes and the Persians, no decree made by the king could be changed.

So Daniel was condemned to be cast into the den of lions, but the king said,

"Thy God, whom thou servest continually, he will deliver thee."

Then a stone was laid over the mouth of the den, and the king sealed it with his own signet, and with that of his lords, that the purpose might not be changed.

That was a long night for Darius the king. He could neither eat nor sleep, and he would hear no music, but very early in the morning he went to the den of the lions and with a very sorrowful voice cried:

"O Daniel, servant of the living God! is thy God whom thou servest continually able to deliver thee from the lions?"

Then up from the pit came a strong, cheery voice saying:

"O king, live forever! My God hath sent his angel, and hath shut the lions mouths, that they have not hurt me."

Then there was joy in the king's heart and he had Daniel brought up out of the den, and no hurt was found upon him, because he had believed in God, but the men who had accused Daniel were cast into the lions' den and destroyed.

Darius acknowledged the God of Daniel before all his kingdom, and commanded the people to honor Him, so that Daniel and his people suffered no more from their enemies during the reign of Darius. After the death o Darius, Cyrus was made king of Persia, and he also was kind to Daniel. The Lord gave him a tender heart toward the captives of Judah who had been in his land for seventy years, so that he sent them back into their own land and helped them to rebuild their city and their Temple

CHAPTER XXXIII.

THE STORY OF JONAH.

More than eight hundred years before the birth of Christ a prophet named Jonah lived in the land of Israel. He had given the Lord's messages to his own people, and they had listened to them, and a part of their country had been saved by obeying the Word of the Lord as it was brought to them by Jonah.

But when the Lord wished to send Jonah to warn a great city in Assyria to repent of their sins, he did not wish to go. Nineveh was a very old and a very great city. It was built soon after the flood, but was still at a high point of glory and wealth in the time of Jonah.

It was a heathen city, but God is the Father of all who live, and cares for all His children, though they may not know or care for Him.

Perhaps Jonah was afraid, for the people were strong and warlike, and they would not wish to hear about their wickedness. So Jonah ran away to the sea shore and took a ship from Joppa to go to Tarshish. He had not gone far from shore when a storm of wind rose, and the wind tossed the ship on the great angry waves until it was very nearly wrecked

The men were afraid, and each prayed to his God, and threw out the goods they were carrying in order to make the ship lighter.

Where was Jonah? He was below the decks asleep. When the captain found him he cried out,

"What meanest thou, O sleeper? Arise, call upon thy God, if so be that God will think upon us, that we perish not."

Then they began to wonder if the storm had not been sent upon them for the wickedness of some one in the ship, and they cast lots to see who it could be. The lot fell upon Jonah. Then they asked Jonah his name and country, and of his journey. He told them all about it. Then the men were more afraid, for they knew that he had tried to run away from the Lord, and they said,

"What shall we do unto thee, that the sea may be calm unto us?"

"Take me up and cast me forth into the sea," he said, "so shall the sea be calm unto you, for I know that for my sake this great tempest is upon you."

It was not easy for the men, who were kind-hearted, to throw into the sea a man so honest and so willing to die, so they rowed very hard, and tried their best to reach the shore, but they could not. So they prayed to Jonah's God to forgive them, and then threw Jonah into the sea.

But the Lord meant not only to teach Jonah a lesson, but to teach, through Jonah, a lesson to His children who should live in the ages to come. He was to make him also a sign of the coming Christ.

When Jonah believed he was sinking down into the green depths of the sea to die, a great fish, prepared by the Lord, opened his mouth and took him in. We cannot understand all the ways of God, but we know that "nothing is impossible with God," and that he was able to keep his servant alive even in such a strange place as this.

For three days and three nights he was kept in his living prison, and was able to pray to God, and to know where he was.

"The waters compassed me about," he said, "even to the soul; the depth closed me round about, the weeds were wrapped about my head. I went down to the bottoms of the mountains; the earth with her bars was about me forever."

Then he praised and thanked God, for he knew that he meant to save him. And when the Lord spoke to the fish, it threw Jonah out upon the dry land.

The second time Jonah heard the voice of the Lord telling him to go to Nineveh and preach the words that should be given him to say, and this time he obeyed.

It was a long journey to Nineveh, and when Jonah reached it he found that the city was so great that it would take three days to walk around the walls.

JONAH THROWN ON THE DRY LAND.

The walls were a hundred feet high. And so broad that three chariots could be driven on them side by side. The walls had fifteen hundred towers, each two hundred feet high. Inside the walls lived hundreds of thousands of people, many of them rich merchants or princes and nobles who lived in palaces, and thought only of their own pleasure and glory. They had grown very selfish and wicked.

When Jonah had walked a day's journey into the city, he began to cry in the streets the message God had given him,

"Yet forty days, and Nineveh shall be overthrown!"

The people began to tremble and be afraid of the strange voice that went up and down the long streets crying out these terrible words. They began to believe in Jonah's God, and to repent.

They repented in the eastern way, by putting on a garment of coarse sackcloth, and sitting in ashes. All did this, even to the king, who took off his beautiful robes and sat down in ashes before the Lord. He also proclaimed a fast to all the people, and urged them to "turn every one from their evil way."

When the Lord saw that they turned away from their sins, for He could look into their hearts, and read all their thoughts, He was satisfied, and said he would not destroy Nineveh.

But Jonah, who could not read the hearts of men, was not satisfied. He was very angry. He wanted to have the Ninevites see that he was a true prophet, for if no destruction came upon them he feared that they might call him a false prophet. So he complained to God, and said,

"Now, O Lord, take, I beseech Thee, my life from me, for it is better to die than to live!"

The Lord's gentle word to Jonah was,

"Doest thou well to be angry?"

Jonah went outside the city walls, and made for himself a little house of the branches of trees and waited to see if the city would be destroyed. It was very hot and Jonah was deeply troubled, and the Lord, who is full of love and pity for His children, caused a gourd vine with large leaves to spring up and grow over the dried branches of the little house that sheltered Jonah, and he was very glad and grateful. But the Lord, who always looks upon the heart, saw that the heart of Jonah was not yet wholly right, and the next morning he allowed a worm to eat the gourd until it withered. Then the sun beat down upon Jonah's head until he fainted and wished to die, saying, as he had said before,

"It is better for me to die than live!"

But the Lord was patient with him, and said,

"Doest thou well to be angry for the gourd?"

And Jonah replied ungraciously,

"I do well to be angry, even unto death."

Then the Lord in his love and pity answered,

"Thou hast had pity on the gourd, for the which thou hast not labored, neither madest it grow; which came up in a night and perished in a night; and should not I spare Nineveh, that great city, wherein are more than sixscore thousand persons that cannot discern between their right hand and their left hand, and also much cattle?"

Jonah did not know all that was in the mind of the Lord, though he was a prophet. He did not know that he was one of the signs of the Lord's first coming, for Jesus spoke of Jonah as a "sign," that as he was three days and three nights within the great fish "so shall the Son of man be three days and three nights in the heart of the earth."

CHAPTER XXXIV.

ESTHER, THE QUEEN.

About five hundred years before Christ King Ahasuerus (Xerxes) reigned over Persia. In the third year of his reign he gave a royal feast to all the princes and nobles of Persia and Media, in Shushan, the royal city. It lasted one hundred and eighty days, and was very costly, for the king wished to show the great men from all his provinces the riches and glory of his kingdom and of his palace.

At the end of these days he made another feast to all who were in Shushan, a feast of seven days, and which included great and small. The palace garden was hung with awnings of white and green and violet, fastened with cords and silver rings to pillars of marble.

Wine was given to the guests in golden cups as they sat on couches of gold and silver, and the pavement of the court was of many colored marbles.

In another part of the palace Vashti, the queen, also made a feast for the women.

On the seventh day the king sent his seven chamberlains to bring Queen Vashti before him, wearing her royal crown. He wished to show to his people and princes the beauty of the queen, for she was very fair to look upon.

But the queen refused to obey the king's command, and he was angry. He asked the seven princes who stood next to him in the kingdom what he should do, and what the laws of the Medes and Persians (which could not be broken) would say in such a case.

The princes did not speak of any law, but one of them told the king that the conduct of Vashti would do them great harm through all the kingdom, for women hearing of the act of the queen, would despise and disobey their husbands. They advised, therefore, that a commandment should go forth from the king and be written among the laws of the Medes and Persians, that Vashti should no more come before the king, and that her royal estate should be given to another better than she.

This pleased the king, and he did as Memucan, the prince, had advised, and he sent letters into all parts of his empire to people of various languages, that every man should rule in his own house.

Then the king's servants, the nobles, advised the king to send officers to every part of his kingdom to find some one worthy to take the place of Queen Vashti, and the plan pleased the king, and he did so.

There was in Shushan a Jew named Mordecai, who had been brought away from Jerusalem with the captives when Nebuchadnezzar conquered the city. He had an adopted daughter named Hadassah. This was her true name, although the Persians called her Esther. She was the daughter of Mordecai's uncle, and when her father and mother died, Mordecai took her for his own. She was very beautiful, and as good as she was beautiful, for Mordecai had taught her to be faithful to the true God, though living among a strange people.

When Mordecai heard that the king was seeking for a maiden worthy to be a queen through all his provinces, he brought Esther and placed her in care of Hegai, who had the care of that part of the king's house where the women lived. Hegai was very kind to her, and gave her seven maids to serve her, and the best place in the house for her own.

Mordecai had told Esther not to speak of her Jewish family, but every day he walked before the court of the women's house to ask how she did and what had become of her.

Out of all the maidens brought from the city and the kingdom Esther was chosen by the king to be queen in the place of Vashti, and he placed the royal crown upon her head, and proclaimed a great feast that he called Esther's feast, when he gave gifts and made a holiday for all the people to rest and be happy in all his provinces.

Mordecai sat daily at the king's gate, and once while there he heard of a plot to kill the king by two of his chamberlains, and he sent word secretly to Esther, and she told the king in Mordecai's name, so that these two men were hanged, and the account of it was written in the king's book of records.

About this time the king gave great honors to a man named Haman. He set him above all his princes, and when the king's servants who were at his gate knew it they all bowed down and gave great honor to Haman, whenever he passed, for the king had so commanded them; but Mordecai would not bow to Haman. When Haman saw this he was full of anger toward Mordecai the Jew, and he made a wicked plan to destroy not only Mordecai, but all his people.

So he came with wily ways and cunning speech to the king, saying,

"There is a certain people scattered abroad and dispersed among the people in all the provinces of thy kingdom, and their laws are diverse from from all people, neither keep they the king's laws, therefore it is not for the king's profit to suffer them. If it please the king let it be written that they be destroyed, and I will pay ten thousand talents of silver to the hands of those that have the charge of the business, to bring it into the king's treasuries."

Then the king gave his ring to Haman as a sign that he would pledge his word to do what he asked, and said,

"The silver is given to thee, the people also, to do with them as it seemeth good to thee."

Then Haman had letters written and sealed with the king's seal ring, saying to the rulers of every province in the kingdom that all Jews, both young and old, throughout the kingdom, must be destroyed in one day, and their goods, and money, and lands be taken for a prey, and the thirteenth day of the twelfth month was set in which to destroy them.

After the messengers were sent out the king and Haman sat down to drink wine, but the city was troubled.

Then Mordecai rent his clothes in sign of mourning, and went out into the streets of the city clothed in sack-cloth uttering a loud and bitter cry. He cried even before the king's gate.

All through the kingdom there was great mourning among the Jews, and they fasted and wept in sack-cloth and ashes.

When Esther heard that Mordecai was clothed in sack-cloth she was deeply grieved, and sent some garments to clothe him, but he would not receive them. Then she sent for the king's chamberlain Hatach, and gave him a command to Mordecai to tell what caused his grief.

Hatach found him at the king's gate, and Mordecai told him all that had happened to him, and of the great sum of money that Haman had promised to pay into the king's treasuries for the Jews to destroy them. He also gave him a copy of the decree to show Esther, and told Hatach to charge her that she go before the king and make request for her people.

Hatach took these words to Esther, and Esther sent a reply by Hatach, saying that it was known in all the king's palace that no man or woman could come into the king's presence in the inner court who had not been called, and for any who so entered there was but one law, and that was that they be put to death, unless the king hold out to them the golden sceptre. She had not been called to see the king, she said, in thirty days.

Hatach gave this message to Mordecai, and he again sent word to Esther that she could not hope to escape the decree, as she too was of the Jews. He told her that deliverance must come to the Jews in some other way, but she and her family would be destroyed, and then he added,

"Who knoweth whether thou art come to the kingdom for such a time as this?"

Then Esther made her resolve, and sent word to Mordecai to gather all the Jews in Shushan together to fast night and day, while she and her maidens fasted also.

"And so I will go in unto the king," she said, "which is not according to the law, and if I perish, I perish."

And Mordecai went his way and did as Esther had commanded.

It was the third day when Esther arose from her fast before the Lord and put on her beautiful royal robes and stood in the inner court of the king's house in sight of the royal throne.

When the king saw Esther standing in the inner court he was not displeased, but his heart was turned toward her, and he held out to her the golden sceptre that was in his hand.

"What wilt thou, Queen Esther?" he said, "and what is thy request? it shall be even given thee to the half of the kingdom."

HAMAN DENOUNCED BY THE QUEEN.

"If it seem good unto the king," said Esther, "let the king and Haman come this day unto the banquet that I have prepared for him."

So the king commanded Haman, and they came to the queen's banquet. The king knew that Esther had a favor to ask of him, so he said again:

"What is thy petition? and it shall be granted thee; and what is thy request? even to the half of the kingdom it shall be performed."

But Esther was wise. She begged as her petition and request that the king and Haman would come to the banquet she should prepare the next day also, and she would then do as the king had said.

Haman went home very happy and proud that he had been so honored by the queen, and told his wife and his friends of all the glory and honor that had come to him.

"Yet all this availeth me nothing," he said, "so long as I see Mordecai the Jew sitting at the king's gate."

Then his wife and his friends urged him to build a high gallows and ask the king on the next day to hang Mordecai upon it. "Then go thou merrily with the king unto the banquet," they added.

This pleased Haman, and he ordered the gallows to be made.

That night the king was restless, and he could not sleep, and he commanded that the book of records be brought and read aloud to him. Then he found that it was written that Mordecai had saved the king's life when it was threatened by his two chamberlains.

"What honor and dignity hath been done to Mordecai for this?" he asked, and his servants replied:

"There is nothing done for him."

"Who is in the court?" cried the king. Now Haman had come in to speak to the king to have Mordecai hanged.

"Haman standeth in the court," said the king's servants, and the king said,

"Let him come in."

As Haman came in the king said,

"What shall be done to the man that the king delighteth to honor?"

Haman thought in his heart, "To whom would the king delight to do honor more than to myself," and then he replied, thinking all the time of himself.

"For the man whom the king delighteth to honor let the royal apparel be brought which the king useth to wear, and the horse that the king rideth upon, and the crown royal which is set upon his head, and let this apparel and horse be delivered to the hand of one of the king's most noble princes, that they may array the men withal whom the king delighteth to honor, and bring him on horseback through the street of the city, and proclaim before him, 'Thus shall it be done to the man whom the king delighteth to honor.'"

Then the king said, "Make haste, and take the apparel and the horse as thou hast said, and do even so to Mordecai, the Jew, that sitteth at the king's gate; let nothing fail of all that thou hast spoken."

Haman did as he was commanded, for he could do nothing else, and after it was all over Mordecai took his place again at the king's gate, but Haman hastened home mourning, and with his head covered.

The next day he came to the queen's banquet with the king, and again the king said,

"What is thy petition, Queen Esther? and it shall be granted thee; and what is thy request? and it shall be performed, even to the half of my kingdom."

Then the queen made her request, saying,

"If I have found favor in thy sight, O king, and if it please the king, let my life be given me at my petition, and my people at my request; for we are sold, I and my people, to be destroyed, to be slain, and to perish. But if we had been sold for bondmen and bondwomen I had held my tongue, although the enemy could not countervail the king's damage."

"Who is he, and where is he," cried the king, "That durst presume in his heart to do so?"

Then Esther said, "The adversary and enemy is this wicked Haman."

Haman was overcome with fear at this, and the king was so angry that he rose up and went out into the palace garden. Haman stood up to make a plea for his life, and when the king came in he found Haman fallen at the queen's feet.

One of the king's chamberlains who knew what the king wished told him of the gallows at Haman's house that had been made for Mordecai, and the king said, "Hang him thereon," and they did so, and the king's anger was pacified.

That day the king gave Haman's house to the queen. Mordecai came before the king that day also, for Esther had told him how he was related to her, and the King gave to Mordecai the ring that he had once given to Haman. Esther's petition was not yet finished, so she fell down at the king's feet and asked for the life of her people, and that the decree might be changed.

Then the king held out his golden sceptre to Esther, and she arose. She spoke noble words of petition for her people, and the king told Mordecai to write in the king's name and seal with the king's seal letters that should make the decree void.

So the scribes were called in and the letters were written and sealed with the king's ring, and sent out to every province in the kingdom.

Mordecai went out of the palace that day clothed in royal garments of violet and white, fine linen and purple, and a great crown of gold upon his head, and there was joy in Shushan, and there was joy among the jews all over the land. They hanged the ten sons of Haman, and destroyed their enemies by the king's permission, so that they had rest from persecution. They also set apart two days for a feast of thanksgiving through all time, and the feast of Purim is kept by all Jews to this day, as it was first confirmed by the decree of Esther.

And Mordecai was next to the king and honored by his brethren the Jews as long as he lived, for he always sought their peace, and was as a father to them.

www.ingramcontent.com/pod-product-compliance
Lightning Source LLC
Chambersburg PA
CBHW020055170426
43199CB00009B/291